Rethinking the End of the World

Rethinking the End of the World

Understanding Apocalyptic Spirituality

B. L. Cooper

Foreword by Don Thorsen

RESOURCE *Publications* · Eugene, Oregon

RETHINKING THE END OF THE WORLD
Understanding Apocalyptic Spirituality

Resource Publications
An Imprint of Wipf and Stock Publishers
199 W. 8th Ave., Suite 3
Eugene, OR 97401

www.wipfandstock.com

ISBN 13: 978-1-4982-2441-3

Manufactured in the U.S.A.   05/11/2015

This book is dedicated to my amazing family with whom I shared in this work. Without their support, encouragement, and sacrifice of time with me, this book would have never been created.

Contents

Figure

Foreword

Apocalyptic Spirituality

TOO OFTEN PEOPLE READ apocalyptic literature for what it may tell them about the future, while they fail to recognize and put into practice what apocalyptic literature has to say about Christian living right now. B. L. Cooper writes an important book about the Book of Revelation and other apocalyptic literature, for example, as found in Jesus' parables and Paul's letters, regarding their teachings about spiritual formation, Christian discipleship, and their relevance here-and-now for people, individually and collectively.

In discussing *apocalyptic spirituality*, Cooper draws out essential teachings from eschatological literature in Scripture about how Christians ought to live faithfully, hopefully, and lovingly in the present. Such literature provides vital instruction on how individuals may grow in personal as well as spiritual maturity. Most people do not look at the Book of Revelation, for example, as a spiritual guide for their present lives, but through their neglect, they miss out on a rich resource for Christian living.

People often overlook the spiritual resources in apocalyptic literature because they become preoccupied with the future. They study the Book of Revelation in order to interpret the signs of the times, seek out prophesied events, and perhaps predict the precise end of the world. In Matthew 24, Jesus said that no one knows the day and the hour of the end times, and that people should focus upon being always ready for Jesus' second coming. Yet, Christians become engrossed with the future, sometimes becoming so obsessed with speculation that they neglect their present lives. They neglect their spiritual well-being, their love for God, and their love for neighbors.

Cooper uses personal stories and stories from church history in order to expose those zealots preoccupied with the future, with guesswork about current events, and with their obvious neglect of biblical teachings about Jesus' focus upon godly living here-and-now. There are, of course, tragic stories that can be told about how Christians are sometimes so 'heavenly minded' that they are of 'no earthly good.' Cooper's humor helps readers to laugh as well as learn from apocalyptic doomsayers.

Cooper does not advocate a particular theological view of Christian eschatology. He talks about the different views, but instead focuses upon the spiritual significance of apocalyptic literature, regardless of one's particular eschatology. As such, Christians with any view of the end times will benefit from the nuggets of spirituality Cooper finds in the Book of Revelation and elsewhere in Scripture.

Apocalyptic spirituality has to do with more than personal growth in faith, hope, and love. It is not limited to a kind of spiritual individualism, irrelevant to collective implications for the life of the church, for society, and for the world God created. After all, apocalyptic literature talks about societal, economic, political, and environmental dimensions, more so than other parts of Scripture. Its holism should inspire Christians to focus on issues of justice, advocacy for the poor, and care for the physical world as well as for justification from sin and advocacy for the spiritual dimensions of the world.

Cooper's book begins by talking about the frenetic, helter-skelter, apocalyptic expectations some Christians have, which distract them and others from weighty teachings of Scripture. Such expectations are exciting, and give a triumphal sense of religious certitude. But how certain does God intend Christians to be about predicting the end of the world? By contrast, ought Christians to be more certain with regard to clear-cut biblical teachings about spiritual formation, advocacy for justice, and care for God's creation?

Cooper continues by talking about the nature of apocalyptic literature, its interpretation, and how such literature has been understood and applied throughout church history. Again, stories are told that illuminate the variety of ministries as well as mishaps that arose from Christians' focus on eschatological issues. Although Cooper values the prophetic dimension of apocalyptic literature, he emphasizes its spiritual fruitfulness, too often neglected by Christians.

At the end of his book, Cooper provides numerous suggestions for effectively implementing apocalyptic spirituality taught in the Book of Revelation and other eschatological passages in Scripture. Apocalyptic literature is concerned about people's spiritual well-being; likewise, it is concerned about fighting injustice and the exploitation of God's creation. Regardless of what one expects in the future—whether one expects the world to become worse, better, or maintain some type of status quo—Christians are not exempt from being faithful to all the teachings of Scripture. In other words, they are to love God and to love their neighbors as themselves, and to rely upon the grace of God through the presence and power of the Holy Spirit to live godly, Christ-like lives. Just as Jesus cared for people physically as well as spiritually, we too are to care for them—individually, collectively, holistically.

Cooper convincingly points out that apocalyptic literature has as much to do with our present spiritual well-being as for our future well-being. And that well-being has to do with our spiritual and physical lives, our individual and collective lives, and our environmental and eternal lives. It is my hope that apocalyptic spirituality becomes a more prominent concern in the minds and hearts of Christians as they study and implement the Book of Revelation and other eschatological passages in Scripture. They are as essential to our spiritual formation and Christian living here-and-now as to our eternal life and the consummate manifestation of God's kingdom.

—Don Thorsen

Introduction

The End is Near

They were looking intently up into the sky as he was going, when suddenly two men dressed in white stood beside them. "Men of Galilee," they said, "why do you stand here looking into the sky? This same Jesus, who has been taken from you into heaven, will come back in the same way you have seen him go into heaven."

—Acts 1:10–11 NIV

EVER SINCE JESUS LEFT this earth and ascended into heaven, not a generation has gone by that has not wondered and anticipated his return. At times, the anticipation has been so strong that it affects the way we live our lives in positive and even negative ways. The effect of the anticipation for the end of the world on people's spiritual formation is known as apocalyptic spirituality. *Apocalyptic spirituality is the discussion of how people's view of the end of the world and the return of Jesus Christ affects their spirituality on a daily basis in their life today.* Even though apocalyptic spirituality may seem like a new concept to some readers, it is not a new idea. In 1979, Bernard McGinn created a book that was a compilation of works by people who were heavily influenced by the end of the world in the medieval ages that he calls apocalyptic spirituality.[1] As you read this book, I will build on this basic understanding of apocalyptic spirituality and discuss its influence on the spiritual formation of the Christian faith. As we will see in chapter 5, apocalyptic spirituality has influenced many historical events, including the discovery of the "New World." Apocalyptic spirituality can influence people's perspectives on the environment as well and if planting trees is really worth your "limited" time before Jesus returns. Apocalyptic spirituality also influences our political views and can create biases which are motivated by the understanding of end time events that may occur before Jesus comes.

With apocalyptic spirituality being such a great influence on our daily lives as Christians, one would think that the church would consider it an important element on which to often teach and preach. Apocalyptic spirituality is also an important facet of discipleship and influences our spiritual formation as Christians. If I believed that Jesus was coming back tomorrow, then my energies would be focused on the next twenty-four hours. Some of the more fundamental perspectives of the end of the world see anything except evangelism of the gospel a distraction to the church. However, there are other people who feel that Jesus may not come back soon or in this generation, and they are more motivated to plan for long-term spiritual formation. In addition, Christians with a more "far off" perspective consider social justice and environmental issues a huge priority so that they can leave something behind for the generations that will come after us.

So why doesn't the church harness apocalyptic spirituality to help shape the spiritual formation of the church? Part of the reason is because the church is inundated with interpretations. One only needs to spend about five minutes on the Internet googling the book of Revelation to experience the vast amount of opinions and understandings of such a mysterious book. Denominations

---

1. McGinn, *Apocalyptic Spirituality: Treatises and Letters of Lactantius, Adso of Montier-En-Der, Joachim of Fiore, the Franciscan Spirituals, Savonarola*, ed. Richard J. Payne, The Classics of Western Spirituality (Mahwah, NJ: Paulist Press, 1979).

and para-church organizations have been created because of how people thought the end of the world would occur. Wars, genocides, and crimes against humanity have been wrongly justified by certain views and understandings of Revelation. People have given up all of their possessions and gathered together on a hill expecting Jesus to come back because of misunderstandings of the end of the world. This single book at the end of the Bible has played a strong influence in the history of the Christian church. Today, it seems that a majority of Christians either take an extremist view of only accepting one interpretation of Revelation, or they simply don't want to touch the book and read and live all around Revelation but not step foot into its turbulent waters. I've had heated conversations with other Christians who feel my salvation was in jeopardy because I didn't hold the same interpretation as they did. I believe others feel this tension, and while there are some pastors that preach and teach on Revelation, many steer clear of it.

Yet at the same time, it's a money maker. The book of Revelation is filled with fascinating imagery and symbolism. Many books, video games, and movies have been made emphasizing the sensationalism of Revelation and have made millions of dollars. So along with the mystery of understanding this book, you have a section of the media that simply wants to make money off of the sensationalism of it. I even had hesitations about writing on this topic because I was concerned about being stereotyped as someone writing solely to cash in on the sensationalism of Revelation. However, that simply isn't the case.

My passion to write on such a difficult topic comes from a desire to educate the church on a basic understanding of Revelation and the apocalyptic genre of literature in which it was birthed and a basic understanding that creates a spring-board for further interpretation. It is my belief that no matter what eschatological view you hold, we can all come to a common understanding of Revelation: the word of God for his people that is beneficial for the edification of the church and spiritually formative for Jesus' disciples. I believe that there is still a common understanding of the book of Revelation on which Christians can agree no matter what eschatological view each person holds.

My challenge for the reader is to experience a deeper understanding of Revelation, learn how this book can be spiritually formative to your faith today, and begin to rethink the end of the world. By "rethinking" I don't mean that you need to change your interpretation or understanding of the fulfillment of this apocalyptic book. But I want others to come to a primary, basic understanding that creates space for God's mission in the world. I also want others to know how we can co-labor with him on his plans for restoration when Jesus returns for his bride, the church, in whichever way he does choose to return. We will examine the purpose and function of apocalyptic literature, how the book of Revelation has influenced church and society in every generation since Jesus left, and, finally, how we can gain a united agreement of a spiritually formative understanding of Revelation that doesn't change from generation to generation as many of our interpretations do.

So who is this book of Revelation for? This book you are about to read is for anyone who is looking for a practical understanding of Revelation. I do not feel a need to reinvent the wheel. I am not trying to create another academic commentary because I believe there are already some great works out there that don't need to be repeated, but I do believe there is a lack of healthy, practical understandings of Revelation circulating in the twenty-first century.

This book is also designed for small group discussions in order to process the ideas that I put forward from this book in a community setting. My challenge to Christians and churches is to rethink how you view the end of the world and how it affects your spiritual formation today as well as how it prepares the possible future generations that will come after us. So join me as we begin rethinking the end of the world.

1

The Bat Signal

Here I am! I stand at the door and knock. If anyone hears
my voice and opens the door, I will come in and eat with
them, and they with me.

—Rev. 3:20

I LOVE BATMAN! I have been a Batman fan since I was a child. I
loved the story of how a young boy named Bruce Wayne made
the best of a horrible situation when his parents were killed. That
tragic moment in his life was a defining point that led him down a
path of fighting injustice because the city was being overtaken with
crime. An ordinary man became a superhero. He realized that he
was not the only one suffering, but many other people were as well.
So, with his passion to fight for justice and a lot of money at his dis-
posal, Bruce Wayne was able to develop a character that brought
hope to the people of Gotham City: Batman. Whenever the police
commissioner had a problem that was too difficult for the local
law enforcement, he would light up the sky with a spotlight that
projected a figure of a bat, the Bat Signal, and brought hope to a
city of suffering people because they knew a hero was on the way.

WHAT IS APOCALYPTIC LITERATURE?

As we begin our journey together, I can't help but think about the similarities the story of Batman has to the book of Revelation. If you really want to understand Batman, then you have to understand the environment of injustice in Gotham City. And, in the same way, if you want to understand Revelation, then you need to understand apocalyptic literature and the environment in which it was created. Both were created from a need for justice, and both were tools of hope and encouragement during times of oppression. So in comparison, we are going to talk about how Revelation and other apocalyptic writings have been a type of "Bat Signal" to suffering people during the past several thousand years.

Apocalyptic writings were written to address a problem in society.[1] Whenever a major social injustice happened to God's people, they eventually sought to understand it in light of God's promises and covenant. If Israel hadn't experienced severe persecution or exile at any point in their history, then it's possible that apocalyptic literature may never have been created. In the same way, if Bruce Wayne's parents weren't killed and Gotham was a crime-free city, then there would never have been a need for Batman. The goal of apocalyptic literature is to bring restoration to a broken and unjust system. For the Israelites exiled in Babylon, they longed to be restored to their home in Jerusalem and to be a free people again. Batman longed to clean up the streets and eliminate the same injustice that caused great strife in his life as he learned how to grow up without his parents. Although apocalyptic literature can be difficult to understand at times with its imagery and otherworldly analogies, its primary goal is to make the world right again and to create a society that is filled with justice and hope.

For a recent example in our American culture, on September 13, 2001, Jerry Falwell and Pat Robertson, both prominent evangelical preachers, gave an apocalyptic interpretation to the

---

1. Collins, *The Apocalyptic Imagination: An Introduction to Jewish Apocalyptic Literature* , 7.

destruction of the twin towers in New York City on 9/11.[2] While Middle Eastern terrorists organized and carried out the attack, many Americans had difficulty understanding why God would allow such a horrible tragedy to occur. Falwell and Robertson sought to give a spiritual understanding of the physical event that occurred. They described what happened as God lifting the curtain of protection from our country because the United States of America had driven God out of its courts and public school systems. They went so far as to suggest that because of our spiritual immorality as a nation, we deserved it. This was an apocalyptic interpretation because Falwell and Robertson tried to make sense of a national disaster through spiritual means. Their interpretation explained the event as an act of judgment and identified the "evil" parties that caused it. Falwell and Robertson's apocalyptic interpretation of 9/11 was widely condemned by the American people, and both later gave public apologies for their "mis-interpretation." "I hold no one other than the terrorists and the people and nations who have enabled and harbored them responsible for Tuesday's attacks on this nation."[3]

Many early apocalyptic writings were written during the times of Jewish exile in the Old Testament period and later during the Roman occupation of Israel. The Book of Revelation is the most commonly known apocalyptic writing, however, because it is the only book in the biblical canon considered apocalyptic *and* labeled as such. The term revelation in Greek is *apokalypsis,* or apocalypse, revelation, disclosure, or unveiling. Several other apocalyptic writings that aren't included in the Bible are *1st and 2nd Enoch, 4 Ezra, Jubilees, Animal Apocalypse* and the *Similitudes,* just to name a few. There are many different features about these writings that make them apocalyptic. Some of them tell of intense persecution, recollection of past events with a spiritual twist, primordial events, the destruction of the earth, and forms of afterlife. Some even have resurrections in them. The details often change

---

2. Ambinder, Falwell Suggests "Gays to Blame for Attacks." http://abcnews.go.com/Politics/story?id=121322.

3. Ibid.

between the apocalyptic writings, but one feature common to all of them is the presence of judgment and the destruction of the wicked.[4] Like Batman, the Jewish community desired justice and judgment for their oppressors. All of the apocalyptic writings were written at a difficult time in history to give a spiritual explanation for why God was allowing such tragedies to impact God's people.

Apocalyptic writings arose as a "Bat Signal in the sky" over Jewish societies that were suffering great injustices. The overriding idea was that even though bad things were happening, justice was on the way. God could see the evil doers causing the suffering, and they would be judged for it. So, at its very basic level, the book of Revelation serves as a signal in the sky to remind readers and listeners that despite the tribulations being experienced, God is still on the throne, sees the wickedness, and has a plan to bring judgment to the wicked and give rewards to the faithful.

WHY REVELATION IS APOCALYPTIC LITERATURE

Try to imagine the intense environment in the first century when Christians were being persecuted. Roman writers recorded how Nero had Christians crucified and lit on fire to become human torches to provide light for his elaborate parties. Other Christians were dressed in animal skins and thrust into the Roman coliseum with wild animals. When the animals tore them apart, the crowds cheered in their bloodlust. Other Christians were told to declare Caesar as their Lord and renounce Jesus. They were killed if they refused.

Imagine living in such a fearful environment. Even the twelve apostles were persecuted and killed. According to church tradition, the only apostle who lived to die a natural death after escaping several attempts on his life was the apostle John, and he was thought to be exiled to the island of Patmos as a prisoner. Imagine what he witnessed as his fellow apostles, each one a close friend,

4. Collins, 41.

were martyred for their faith in Jesus Christ. From this perspective, the book of Revelation could not have come at a more opportune time when a newly founded church was struggling to grow in an intensely hostile environment. Revelation shone as a "Bat Signal" to a persecuted church that reminded every Christian who was wondering if "this" was all worth it and that God had a plan. It reminded the persecuted church that God is still on the throne, and Jesus promised to return and bring justice to a world that was evil and unjust to his people. Imagine how refreshing it must have been to the early church to hear Revelation being read and to be reminded that God was with his people, and he had a plan.[5] If they remained faithful during this difficult tribulation, then God would reward them with an eternal dwelling where no more tears would be shed and all is at peace. Revelation served as a reminder that the refining fire being put to their faith was not in vain. God would prevail, and one day they would be rewarded for their perseverance as followers of Jesus Christ.

WHAT IS APOCALYPTIC SPIRITUALITY?

Although it is hard to give an exact definition of "spirituality" because there are so many out there, a Christian understanding of this term involves the inner workings of a person's soul—a person's entire self.[6] From a Christian perspective, this refers to the inner soul's experience of connecting to the God of the Bible. Therefore, apocalyptic spirituality is how a person's soul seeks to connect to God in light of the apocalypse, such as a belief that the world will end. Within the realm of apocalyptic spirituality, we have a very broad spectrum of understandings depending on how imminently

5. Most people in the ancient world were illiterate and most likely heard Revelation rather than reading it for themselves. Revelation was also sent to the "seven churches of Asia Minor" as a circuit route so that it could be read to a large number of Christians.

6. There are multiple Christian views of the soul, and I do not intend to deal with those views. Suffice it to say that language of the soul is biblical, and it is often used to talk about a person's essential selfhood.

people feel the end of the world will arrive. For example, how would you spend your time differently with God if you knew that the world was coming to an end tomorrow? You would probably quickly make a plan of events, and at all haste, seek to fulfill those actions as quickly as possible to make sure that everything is in sorts before Jesus returns. Some groups and churches tend to shy away from long-term social justice projects because it can be a "distraction" from the immediate work of the gospel in light of Jesus coming back at any moment. Nineteenth-century evangelist D.L. Moody once said, "I don't find any place where God says that the world is to grow better and better . . . I look upon this world as a wrecked vessel; God has given me a lifeboat and said to me, 'Moody, save all you can.'"[7] This view has become popular in many evangelical circles that see the world as a wrecked ship and not worth the time and effort to save. Oftentimes, this is expressed as a lack of interest in participating in matters of justice, or creation care ministries and other causes that support the environment.

Conversely, how would you spend your time if you knew for a fact that Jesus wasn't going to return in your life time? How serious would you take your faith? The socially conscious ministries in the world today tend to invest large amounts of energy and resources into long-term projects that may outlast their lifetime. For example, the Eden Projects is a present-day Christian organization with the goal of reforesting Ethiopia, Madagascar, and Haiti.[8] This is an ambitious environmental goal that doesn't feel the weight of an impending doom for the end of the world. The apocalyptic spirituality of Eden Projects does not see the world as a sinking ship that needs to be deserted, but instead is concerned about the longevity of the ship and its sustainable environments for the peoples of the world. How people view the end of the world affects how they live their lives today. Perhaps it is time to rethink the end of the world so that we can develop healthy discipleship and Christian living through apocalyptic spiritual formation.

7. Williams, *The Life and Work of Dwight L. Moody: The Great Evangelist of the 19th Century* , 149.

8. www.edenprojects.org

THE NEED FOR APOCALYPTIC SPIRITUAL FORMATION

One of the many challenges of understanding Revelation has been in relating it to a culture that isn't being persecuted. For the early church that was experiencing tribulation and persecution, it was a scroll of hope that was directly applicable to their immediate situation. However, Emperor Constantine changed the game in the fourth century by making a decree that Christianity was to be an imperial religion. Christians stopped interpreting it as literally and began interpreting it more allegorically because the church was no longer being persecuted. Later in chapter 5, we will glimpse at the past two thousand years of how this apocalyptic book of Revelation affected the spirituality of Christians; we have to admire their desire to understand Revelation within their current context.

The interpretations of Revelation have changed dramatically over these past two thousand years because each generation has been trying to apply it to their current lives and society. But surely, isn't there a way to interpret this book on a basic level that helps us to understand God and his plan for his kingdom that doesn't change from generation to generation? It can be tiring and spiritually exhausting having to change your eschatological view every time there is a natural disaster or a change in world politics.

Historically, the church has been somewhat divided when it comes to its interpretation and use of Revelation. For example, when people were under heavy persecution or tribulation, they were able to relate to Revelation in a way that helped them understand God's grace and mercy in the midst of their persecution. A persecuted church's focus of interpretation was toward perseverance and spiritual formation as they strove to remain righteous despite the temptations to cave in to the cultural persecution. The Bat Signal of Revelation was a reminder in the sky that while things on earth were spinning out of control and it was hard to find peace amidst all the suffering, there was a God in heaven who was looking down upon them and taking notes on how his people were being treated.

Conversely, when Christianity is prosperous and doesn't experience tribulations and persecution, Revelation may become an informational road map that explains when future persecution and tribulation will occur. All of the comforts that are afforded a persecuted church suddenly become a "guidebook" and may lose its sense of personal connection with God's mission and message. In more recent cases, if persecution isn't present in Christianity, then the church creates a future plan for persecution in order to be able to relate to Revelation. However, without real persecution, there is little reason or spiritual friction to strive for righteousness. Therefore, the focus on eternal life becomes the prize. With eternal life as the prize, there seems to be little to do "while the church waits" for the return of Jesus or the hour of death. Spiritual formation in the form of discipleship can be minimized, and evangelism is relegated to simply saving people from a sinking ship. Church history is a tug-of-war between these two views, at least, as Christians enter and exit periods of persecution. Yet, for some people groups around the world, persecution has seldom left.

Nevertheless, there is a constant thread of spiritual formation that runs through Revelation that is often overlooked by the sensational interpretations that look for signs and apocalyptic timelines. John Hagee's *Four Blood Moons: Something Is About to Change* is an example of this sensational interpretation.[9] Hagee writes about how rare it is that God is aligning Scripture, science, and history to show us the signs of the end times. However, Hagee's application is merely to make sure that we are simply watching and listening to these messages. There is no deeper call to character formation as a disciple of Jesus Christ. Instead, we are called deeper into the sign-seeking and sensationalism of end time's speculation that leads to watching more TV and reading more books about when the end will come.

Believers need to understand the importance of apocalyptic spiritual formation because it will help us grow deeper in our relationship with God and connects us to all who are suffering in the world today. Revelation is more than just a book of signs and

9. Hagee, *Four Blood Moons: Something Is About to Change* .

chronological roadmaps. Revelation is a book about the heart of God to bring justice and spiritual strength for his suffering children. It is a book that shows us God's mission and final plan for both reconciliation and restoration.

WHAT ARE WE GOING TO DO ABOUT IT?

Revelation's purpose is to provide a "message in the sky" that God is present in our struggles in this world, and he has a plan for our future redemption. Revelation shows us the very heart of God and his desire for his people. It is in this plan and concern from God that we find hope. So we as believers must ask ourselves the question: What are we going to do about it? Are we going to say, "That's nice," and set Revelation on the shelf until the day of suffering comes? Or perhaps we'll sit down and create a plan that will cause us to suffer so that Revelation will then relate to us? Or could we use its message to understand God's heart and plan for those in the world who are persecuted or suffering and then co-labor with God to bring justice to their circumstances? Perhaps we could even display Revelation in the sky to them as a message of hope and present restoration that God sees them, and he is still on the throne and is making note of who is oppressing them. Perhaps Revelation is more relevant to the world today than we ever could have imagined.

2

The Carrot or the Whip

You have persevered and have endured hardships for my
name, and have not grown weary.

—Rev. 2:3

WHENEVER I HEAR THE idiom of the carrot or a stick, I imagine a
boy sitting on a cart trying to get his donkey, which is harnessed
to the cart, to move forward. The boy has two options from which
to choose. First, he could use a common method of making the
donkey move by whipping it to make it move forward out of fear
and pain. The second option is to tie a carrot to the end of a stick
and then hold it out in front of the donkey. Hopefully, the carrot
will motivate the animal to move forward out of hunger or a desire
to get the reward, which is the carrot.

Just like the donkey in the story, people today can become
complacent in this life by enjoying what is around them and set
up a camp of spiritual stubbornness. In this case, people can feel
unmotivated to improve their spiritual life because they enjoy
things where they are. However, if people begin to feel the whip
and believe that life isn't that great and begin to desire something

better, then they may move forward in their spiritual formation by searching for a way to ease their pain or escape their current tribulation. However, people may also move forward because of a reward they see in front of them. If they value the prize more than what they currently have, then they will begin to move forward to grab hold of the prize.

RESISTANCE IS FUTILE, YOU SHALL BE SPIRITUALLY FORMED

Spiritual formation is inevitable. Dallas Willard notes that spiritual formation is the shaping and reshaping of the inner life," and "is a process that happens to everyone. The most despicable as well as the most admirable of persons have had a spiritual formation. Terrorists as well as saints have had a spiritual formation. Their spirits or hearts have been formed. Period."[1] Just as the donkey has a choice to move or not move, so people choose daily how they will be formed spiritually—consciously or unconsciously, intentionally or unintentionally. Choosing not to move also shapes a person spiritually.

How people view the end of the world may affect their spiritual formation today. The beginning illustration shows us two basic motivations for spiritual formation: punishment (suffering) and reward (blessing). Understanding these two reasons for spiritual change in our lives will help us to see how the book of Revelation can affect our spiritual formation more than two thousand years after it was written.

THE WHIP

The nature of hope is that it is found in the absence of possession. A rich man, for example, does not hope to become rich if he is already wealthy. A man does not hope to be married after he says

1. Willard, *Renovation of the Heart: Putting on the Character of Christ* , 10, 19.

his wedding vows. When something is desired and is absent of possession, hope takes flight and gives the strength to persevere. In regard to Revelation, it is commonly believed that Revelation was written during a time when Christians were being persecuted by Jews and Romans. If this is true, then you can imagine the hope the message of Revelation gave to those suffering saints. With the whip of suffering at their backs, they had the hope to carry on, to move forward, because Revelation taught them about a future relationship with the God for whom they were suffering.

In times of great suffering, Christianity has often flourished because a powerful element in Christianity is hope. The death and resurrection of Jesus is the single greatest victory in the history of the world—a victory of the eternal over the temporal. The unwavering hope for a better quality of life, or eternal life, has kept the suffering moving forward and focusing their spiritual formation on the future hope that God will bring justice and reward them with eternal peace for their suffering.

However, if "peace and prosperity" is experienced in this present world, then people are tempted to choose the comforts *now* instead of "waiting" for them in eternity. And if they are experiencing their comfort now, then Christ-like spiritual formation is not required to get what they desire . . . peace, comfort, and prosperity in this world. So, for Christ-like spiritual formation to occur, there must be a transition from the temporal to the eternal. If there is no transition in the present life, then apocalyptic spirituality can have a negative influence on spiritual formation. For example, "turn or burn" theology, which has its own shock value, seeks to communicate a sense of future suffering but does not engage the person in the world today other than to save the person from eternal torment.

"Turn or burn" theology and preaching recognizes the spiritual formation of apocalyptic spirituality and uses it as a tool for conversion. Many people have experienced "turn or burn" theology and preaching as a person standing in a public area with a bullhorn announcing to the masses that they need to repent or they will go to hell. This style of "evangelism" is designed to motivate people to repent from their present reality of prosperity, and subsequently be spiritually formed into Christ-likeness so that they will be saved from a future potential form of suffering. In a culture that isn't experiencing persecution, this form of evangelism creates a fear of future suffering in order to create Christ-like spiritual formation for today.[2] The danger of such evangelism is in the motivation for conversion simply to secure a future placement in heaven, rather than motivating the person to desire to be a member of the present and earthly kingdom of God. This form of evangelism encourages people to belong to the future kingdom of God in order to simply reserve a spot in eternity and to receive a *Get Out of Hell Free* card. However, there is little motivation to transform the world around them or continue to grow deeper in their own spiritual journey because they have managed to escape the future suffering that caused them to join the kingdom of God in the first place. Such spirituality is a dangerous and stagnant place to be.

Likewise, some end time interpretations create future possibilities of great persecution, and therefore gives a call to repentance in order to be "saved" from future trials and tribulations. It's true that the book of Revelation was birthed in a time of tribulation in the early church and that apocalyptic literature served as a sign in the sky that God was on the way and hope was around the corner, despite their suffering. However, when the message of Revelation is taken out of that context, it is like a fish out of water, and people don't immediately know how to deal with it. Current end time theories, timelines, and maps seek to put the fish back in the water by creating elaborate conspiracy theories and timeline maps that create future persecutions that will once again make the book of Revelation relevant to a "prosperous" culture. Although I admire those—pastors and scholars—who make such end time interpretations out of a desire to help non-persecuted people relate to this book, the great tragedy is that the future prophesies espoused by

2. According to James Fowler, fear may serve as a psychological motivation, which contributes to religious conversion. Of course, there occur other psychological motivations that may affect people's conversion experiences. See Fowler, *Stages of Faith: The Psychology of Human Development and the Quest for Meaning*, 117–34, 269–91.

them distract the church from becoming a more restorative agent of change in the world today.

Because there is such an emphasis on relieving future suffering instead of present day spiritual formation, some Christians are against environmental activity (and other acts of justice and compassion) because they believe it to be a distraction from converting people to Christianity.[3] They go so far as to refer to environmentalism as the "green dragon," which calls upon imagery from the book of Revelation.[4] These people are so focused on the imminent return of Jesus and focus so much time and energy on watching the signs to "be ready" for future events in their own spirituality that they eliminate themselves from becoming catalysts for restorative change of all aspects of life for which Jesus was concerned in the world we live in today. They are like passengers of a cruise ship that are all lined up on the dock, luggage in tow, but there is no ship in sight. While others around them are working to make the docks a better place to be—spiritually and physically—and investing in the future of the docks, these passengers stubbornly refuse to get out of line because that is not the focus of their reality. Their focus is on a future reality. In the meantime, there are millions of Christians (and others too) around the world enduring persecution because of their faith, despite how the message of Revelation is wonderfully meaningful and relevant to their current situation. When the church distracts itself by creating scenarios and timelines for possible future persecution, we, too, often miss the opportunity to connect and give hope to generations of Christians suffering for their faith in the world today.

THE CARROT

The other element that causes the donkey referred to earlier to move forward from its position of seeming contentment is the

3. Rudolf, "An evangelical backlash against environmentalism." http://green.blogs.nytimes.com/2010/12/30/an-evangelical-backlash-against-environmentalism

4. The "red dragon"; see Rev. 12:3.

reward of a carrot. The motivation of the donkey to move forward is no longer escapism to get away from pain and suffering, but it voluntarily moves toward something that it desires. The work of moving the cart forward suddenly becomes worth the effort in order to obtain the prize. Likewise, many Western Christians will not exert the effort—facilitated by God's grace—to become people with deep Christ-like character unless the prize before them outweighs their current contentment. Healthy spiritual formation will not occur until a person is motivated to move forward voluntarily, aided by the Holy Spirit and not from some form of perceived escapism.

Although the book of Revelation encourages a persecuted church to persevere through difficult times, people find it hard to apply the book during times of prosperity and contentment. If escape from suffering is the goal and you manage to become free from your oppressors . . . what is left? What do you do then? We can see this dramatic shift in church history when, in 313 CE, Constantine declared Christianity a legal religion by signing the Edict of Milan. Then, in 380 CE, the Edict of Thessalonica declared Christianity as the official state religion. Within a few decades, what was once a small sect in the Roman Empire suffering various levels of persecution was now the declared religion of the entire empire. As a consequence, Revelation transitioned from a book that was most often interpreted literally—due to the change in socio-political context—to a book that was increasingly interpreted allegorically. Suddenly, its message of persevering through persecution didn't make sense in a "Christian Empire." But the question remains: Are literal and allegorical interpretations our only choices when interpreting Revelation? Does it either apply to us or not apply to us? If we are not suffering, then is concocting scenarios that foretell persecution our only option?

This begs the question: Can apocalyptic spirituality motivate a person to become more Christ-like in the absence of persecution and suffering? I believe the answer is yes. The book of Revelation can be relevant to a culture not suffering and still be beneficial for spiritual formation without resorting to scenarios of impending persecution.

Throughout Scripture, Revelation offers one of the most vivid pictures of God's mission in the world. However, many people are standing on the dock, waiting for the ship to arrive when they could be living in the kingdom *today*. Jesus' message of the gospel wasn't "someday" . . . but "The time has come . . . the Kingdom of God is near" (Mark 1:15). It is here. The wait is over. The Kingdom of God is now. Jesus will return one day as promised, but he didn't say we had to wait for the kingdom as well. The greatest thing we can do as a church to apply God's message in Revelation is to further the kingdom here on earth, today, in the same holistic ways Jesus lived and ministered on behalf of the Kingdom of God.

The book of Revelation offers many things to the church in waiting. In the first few chapters, we see a glimpse of how Jesus walks among his churches, an amazing perspective of the throne in heaven, God's heart for the suffering, his desire for justice, and his plan for the restoration of all creation. Although the Western church today may not be able to relate to Revelation as a suffering victim, it can find hope and encouragement in the characteristics of God's kingdom and his plan of restoration for his people. What would it look like if the prosperous church of today was to go into the world to proclaim the good news of this eternal kingdom? I believe the church has two options of application when it comes to the book of Revelation: it can either apply to the world we live in now or wait for a future time when it will apply. I believe that applying it now is our best option.

Imagine the spiritual formation that could happen when the prosperous church prays (and lives, acts) through Revelation with the intent of experiencing the kingdom of God in the world today. Doing this would focus the heart of the church to yearn for the same things for which God yearns. The church could spend time in prayer for the suffering people of the world today who are being persecuted for their faith. The church could pray for justice to be done in the areas of the world where our children are being kidnapped and sold into slavery. Perhaps we could become catalysts for justice through our lives and actions in dark areas where the people have no voice and are defenseless. The reality of Revelation is that the world is full of antichrists (2 John 1:7), but the world is also full of prophets who are willing to lay down their lives for their faith. Imagine a world where the Kingdom of God is active in bold and courageous ways that help bring positive transformation into areas of darkness. Instead, if we simply stand on the docks and wait, then imagine all of the beautiful things we would miss in life.

I believe the carrot of apocalyptic spirituality is the opportunity to participate in bringing the Kingdom of God to those who are suffering in the world today. I believe that because we are not suffering, there is a selfish element to our faith if we do not—by grace—seek the fulfillment of the Kingdom of God. When the prosperous church conjures up future scenarios in which it will be persecuted so that Revelation will become relevant, it becomes a slap in the face to those actually suffering and looking for help today. It is as if the prosperous church exaggerates the pain of a small splinter, while its brothers and sisters in the truly suffering church live in fear of death and torture. How could the church not utilize apocalyptic spirituality to help the suffering church to see the Kingdom of God in practice here and now?

WHAT DRIVES YOUR SPIRITUAL FORMATION?

One of the great ironies concerning apocalyptic spirituality is that what was designed to give hope and perseverance to the suffering church has also been used by the prosperous church to create fear and uncertainty as a way of promoting spiritual formation. This should not be. Once the church is no longer suffering, true apocalyptic spirituality then re-focuses its energies on others who are still suffering. However, when the prosperous church distracts itself by creating future scenarios and confusing timelines, it misses the opportunity to come alongside its brothers and sisters who are still suffering in the world today. It also marginalizes their suffering by asserting that the tribulations identified in Revelation have not begun yet. So we wait on the docks for them to occur.

Focusing on the idiom of the whip or the carrot helps us to understand that Revelation can be beneficial to the church whether it is suffering or prosperous. Although there is an element of waiting in both situations, there is also an element of faith and work on spiritual formation that occurs with either the whip or the carrot. The question is, how will you prepare for the return of Jesus? Are you standing on the dock, looking to the future instead of working—by God's grace—on spiritual formation today?

3

When the Thief Comes

Therefore keep watch, because you do not know the day
or the hour.

—Matt. 25:13

APOCALYPTIC SPIRITUALITY FASCINATED ME as a young Christian
in junior high school. Operation Desert Storm (a war waged by a
U.N.-authorized coalition force from thirty-four nations led by the
United States, against Iraq in response to its invasion and annexa-
tion of Kuwait) was underway. There were many discussions in the
evangelical Christian community about how Saddam Hussein and
Iraq played into the "end times" interpretation of Revelation. One
book I read went into great detail, explaining how we were living
in the end times and that Armageddon was near because Saddam
Hussein was rebuilding the ancient city of Babylon and comparing
himself to Nebuchadnezzar.[1] The authors put their information
alongside the events of Revelation, and I became absolutely convinced I would see Jesus coming back to take us to heaven within
ten years.

1. Dyer and Hunt, *The Rise of Babylon: Sign of the End of Times.*

However, the defeat of the Iraqi forces left me confused because, to my thinking, that was not the way it was supposed to end. The general Christian community around me readily accepted the outcome without much difficulty and began looking to others who might be the next antichrist candidate. Meanwhile, I was confused and offended. I was totally ready for Jesus to come back and take me to heaven and see Revelation fulfilled before my eyes. However, it is now 2014, Saddam Hussein was captured, sentenced to death for his war crimes, and finally executed.

Although I didn't know it at the time, the apocalyptic spirituality I experienced as a teenager greatly affected my spiritual formation. Because I was so fixated on the global events at hand and the uncertainty of the times, my spiritual formation was influenced by being ready and watching the signs for when the Lord would come by to "pick me up." My spiritual development was very self-focused, and although I did warn a few others about the possibility of the Lord coming back, I really wasn't concerned about the transformation of this world, evangelization, or helping others grow spiritually. I was fixated on when Jesus would return, and I wanted to make sure I was going to heaven and not to hell. My apocalyptic spirituality was centered on my own fascination and curiosity with the end of the world.

THE FALL OF THE TEMPLE

Just as Christian understandings of when and how Jesus will return have changed over the years, so has the understanding of what it means to be ready for his return. Some have equated being ready for Jesus' second coming to reading the news, watching world events, and using this information to predict when he will come back. However, many of Jesus' apocalyptic pronouncements were directed toward his contemporaries and were used to announce the final fulfillment of God's judgment and saving work.[2] When we study the apocalyptic passages spoken by Jesus to pronounce

2. Allison et al., *The Apocalyptic Jesus: A Debate*, 24.

judgment on his contemporaries, we see a very different understanding of what it means to be ready.

Chapters 21–25 in the New Testament book of Matthew are excellent examples of Jesus pronouncing an apocalyptic judgment upon his contemporaries. Matthew 21 begins with Jesus visiting the Temple and driving out the money changers who are using areas of the temple for purposes (perhaps unjustly) for which they were not intended (Matt. 21:12–13). Then, as Jesus is on his way to Bethany to spend the night, he pronounces judgment and curses a fig tree for not bearing fruit— in stark comparison to the future judgment, as we will see, of the nation of Israel, and the Temple, in chapter 24, for not producing spiritual fruit (Matt. 21:18–22). The fact that it was a fig tree is significant because it was an Old Testament representation of Israel.[3] The fact that Jesus makes such a judgment on the nation after leaving the Temple shows us that the Temple is the representative heart of the nation's spirituality.

Jesus returns to the Temple the next day and recites a series of parables that concern the proper stewardship of the Temple and the true nature of God's Kingdom. The parables of the two sons (21:28–32), the tenants (21:33–46), the wedding banquet (22:1–14), and paying taxes to Caesar (22:15–22) all criticize how the teachers of the law and religious leaders have been caring for God's place of earthly residence, the Temple. All the while, the Sadducees and Pharisees have been trying to trip up Jesus to give them an excuse to arrest him.

Then in Matthew 22:34, a shift occurs. Jesus goes on the offensive. The Pharisees ask him to name the greatest commandment. In response he tells them the greatest commandment is to love the Lord God with all our heart, soul, mind, and strength, which is the Shema (an affirmation of Judaism and a declaration of faith in one God, Deuteronomy 6:4–5). Jesus then says that the second greatest commandment is like it, which is to love your neighbor as yourself. This second commandment seems to cap off what Jesus saw lacking in the Temple courts . . . loving your

---

3. Osborne, "Matthew," in *Exegetical Commentary on the New Testament*, 770.

neighbor. Then, in response to that lack of effort, Jesus delivers a harsh criticism to the teachers of the law by delivering to them the "seven woes" (Matt. 23:1–38). He calls them out in Old Testament prophet fashion by beginning his public criticism of these religious leaders with the word "woe."[4] He critiques them as hypocrites and seems to hold them to a certain level of responsibility for the lack of spiritual "fruit" he saw in the Temple courts. They didn't love their neighbors; they loved themselves!

In chapter 24, Jesus is leaving the Temple after a long day of teaching and delivering the seven woes to the Temple leadership. He has many things on his mind. Despite all the criticism of the religious leaders and Jesus' concern with the state of the Temple, we see the disciples coming up to Jesus and drawing "his attention to its buildings" (24:1). Despite all that Jesus had encountered the past week inside and around this building, the disciples are still in awe about the outside beauty of the Temple buildings. So it is that Jesus prophesizes its coming destruction: "'Do you see all these things?' he asked. 'I tell you the truth, not one stone here will be left on another; every one will be thrown down'" (24:2). In fact, the Temple was so utterly destroyed that Josephus records it as being leveled to the ground, gutted by fire.[5] Jesus' prophecy of the Temple's destruction has been building up in the preceding verses, ever since the judgment of the fig tree in Matt. 21:18–22. Why would he pronounce such a harsh judgment? The temple was no longer serving its intended purpose much like the fig tree was no longer useful. The fig tree was not able to feed Jesus at a time when he was hungry, and the Temple had failed to feed people spiritually because it was only concerned about feeding itself spiritually and physically. The Temple had become a symbol of abuse and selfishness by the leaders and educators who were supposed to be leading the way in loving God and loving their neighbors.

As the disciples are processing what Jesus is telling them, they ask two questions:

4. Harrington, "Matthew," in *Sacra Pagina*, 326–27.
5. Josephus, *The Jewish War: Revised Edition*, 7.1–3.

1. When will this happen? 24:3b (when the Temple will be destroyed,)

2. What will be the sign of your coming and the end of the age? 24:3b (Jesus' return)

In response, Jesus gives them details about the destruction of the temple and how he will return in complete establishment of God's kingdom. Then, beginning in Matt. 24:36, and through the end of chapter 25, Jesus gives them instructions on how to live until he returns.

THE DAY AND HOUR UNKNOWN

During his discourse in Matt. 24–25, Jesus tells the disciples that not only is the day and hour of his return unknown, but also most people will not even be expecting it (24:42)! Jesus compares the surprise of his return to the suddenness of the flood in the days of Noah (24:37). People were doing just as they pleased right up until the time the flood took them away. They lived according to their own idolatrous and selfish desires. Not only do we not know when he will return, but Jesus implies that he will not tell us because he wants us to be always prepared.

> Therefore, keep watch, because you do not know on what day your Lord will come. But understand this: If the owner of the house had known at what time of night the thief was coming, he would have kept watch and would not have let his house be broken into. So you also must be ready, because the Son of Man will come at an hour when you do not expect him. (Matt. 24:42–44)

Jesus compares himself to a thief breaking into a house and plundering it while the homeowner is asleep, unaware of the activity going on around him.

The hard truth that Jesus communicates is that he doesn't want you to know when he's going to return. If you know when he's coming back, then you won't be ready when he's *not* coming. In other words, if you truly knew for a fact that Jesus was coming back ten years from now, then you would be tempted to "slack off" the first nine years and then get serious about your spiritual formation in the last year. If you know when he's coming back, then of course you'll be ready! However, Jesus doesn't want to come when you're ready, guarded the house, turned on the alarm, and are staying up all night for the burglar to arrive. He wants to see you without your makeup on; he wants to see what you're watching on TV when he pops in for a surprise visit. He wants to see your true character and how you've been formed spiritually right up until the time he returns.

It's also interesting to note the connection between Jesus' words in this passage and his entrance into the Temple, finding the leadership "asleep" and unfruitful. This parable of the thief in the night gives us a glimpse of what Jesus' return will be like. He visited the Temple and left, yet no one realized that God was literally there. He did come like a thief in the night on his first visit, and the amount of people who weren't ready were many. Jesus' criticism of his contemporaries was that they were spiritually asleep and focused on themselves, which led to physical and economic abuses as well as spiritual and religious abuses in that day. Today, we have the opportunity to learn from the mistakes people made from his first visit so that we can be appropriately ready for his second coming.

THE PARABLE OF THE TEN VIRGINS

The parable of the ten virgins (also known as the parable of the wise and foolish virgins) is another story Jesus told to emphasize the importance of being ready for his return. The ten virgins are supposed to take their lamps and go out to meet the bridegroom (Matt. 25:1). Five of the virgins took lamps and oil, while the other five took lamps but no oil. Like everyone else invited to the festivities, they were not told when the bridegroom would arrive and, thus, had to be prepared for a wait. Finally, at midnight—like a thief in the night—the bridegroom suddenly appeared. All ten virgins prepared their lamps, but only five had oil to keep them lit.

The other five weren't prepared to meet the bridegroom and had to leave to buy oil. By the time they returned, it was too late and their entrance into the wedding feast was denied despite their pleas to be granted entrance. The sad truth is that they were given the right information and plenty of time to get what they needed, but were not ready when the bridegroom appeared. Their lack of readiness was their downfall. In similar fashion, the religious leaders caring for the Temple had everything they needed to do the job right and effectively care for their "neighbors" and those in need. But they fell asleep.

THE PARABLE OF THE TALENT

Jesus continues his teaching on the second coming with the parable of the talents (Matt. 25:14–30). It's easy to see in this story the reference to the seven woes spoken against the Temple leadership by Jesus because of their lack of faithfulness as God-honoring stewards of the Temple resources.

The parable of the talents is about a man who went on a long journey, but before leaving entrusted his riches to three servants (v.15). To the first servant, he entrusted five talents; to the second servant three talents, and to the third servant one talent. Even the servant with only one talent of gold wasn't given a small amount. At the time of Jesus, one talent was equivalent to 20.4 kg, or nearly 45 pounds of gold.[6] In today's market, that would be well over one million dollars. Imagine the value at the time of Jesus! The charge given to each man was to use faithfully his time and the talents entrusted to him to increase his master's riches. They were not told when he would return. During the intervening time, the men with five and three talents became actively involved in caring for and investing the gold in their charge. The servant with one talent, however, didn't do anything with the gold given to him. He simply buried it in the ground and waited (v.18). After a long time, the master returned and demanded an accounting from each man

6. Powell, "Weights and Measures," in *Anchor Bible Dictionary*, 908.

of what had been done with his riches (v.19). The first two doubled what had been entrusted to them and were greatly rewarded for their faithfulness (vv.20–23). The master was furious, however, with the third servant who had done nothing with the gold entrusted to him. He had simply buried it, revealing fear and a wrong attitude toward his master and what benefited him. In Luke 19:21, the servant describes the master as unjust. Yet, the servant accepted the master's talent with the expectation of investing it. The master called him "a wicked and slothful servant" for not caring enough to make even the least effort to invest that with which he had been entrusted. Craig Keener argues that banks in the ancient world were not only safe for investments, but that temples (acting as banks) and moneylenders could return a fivefold or even a tenfold yield on investments![7] I often wonder what the man with the one talent did after he buried it. He seemed to have shown no care or obedience for his master's possession, but instead chose to put his time and efforts into his own agenda and investments. There was no effort whatsoever to care for his master's talent, and the unfaithful man was thrown into utter darkness!

Now, let's think about the time and energy the servants with the five and three talents must have put into their investments to double them while their master was away. They must have put lots of thought and effort into endeavors in which they had no direct ownership. After all, they weren't working to increase their own wealth, and the master wasn't obligated to give them much (if anything) in return for their work. Because they knew this, it must have been a very strenuous gesture by each to spend his time and effort for his master's benefit. Yet, when the day of reckoning came, the master rewarded each of them with property of their own to manage. They had been proven faithful while waiting for their master to return home.

The servant who had received the one talent, however, seemed to be motivated by laziness at least, if not also selfish self-interest. Also, the text tells us that he feared his master and therefore buried

7. Keener, *The Gospel of Matthew: A Socio-Rhetorical Commentary* , 147–48.

the gold that was given to him. Even if the servant feared his master, then he could have done far more with the talent he received in order to avoid his master's wrath. In fact, he cared so little for his master's interests that he didn't even bother to deposit the gold in the bank where it could gain interest. No, he simply buried it, put it out of his mind, and selfishly did whatever he wanted to do. Again, we are shown what seems like a comparison that Jesus is making with the teachers of the law and how they have not been caring for the things of God. Jesus himself was in the Temple. The Master had physically returned. Instead of welcoming the Master home, they challenged his authority and later plotted to kill him.

I think it's important to note that these parables about "being ready" for Jesus' return have little to do with watching and worrying about signs—and seem to be more focused on the hearts and attitudes of the people in waiting. Being ready implies that we're prepared for his coming Kingdom, whenever it is, by being faithful stewards of those things we've been entrusted by him with keeping—for his glory, not ours.

THE SHEEP AND THE GOATS

So then, our apocalyptic parables come to a conclusion with the parable of the sheep and the goats. In this story, we are catapulted forward in time to the Day of Judgment and are witnessing Jesus, the Son of Man, dividing all the peoples of the earth into two groups: sheep and goats. The sheep are placed at Jesus' right hand, while the goats are assigned to his left. Jesus then addresses the sheep and welcomes them into his kingdom which, he said, had been prepared for them "from the foundation of the world" (Matt. 25:34). The rest of this narrative is summed up in how people are judged to be sheep or goats and how each group responds to what they're told. Although it seems that Jesus' standard for righteousness in this passage is based on how the peoples of the earth treated their neighbors, it's important to keep this parable in context with the ongoing dialogue that Jesus has been having with the teachers of the law. Jesus says that whoever feeds, cares for, and visits him is found righteous. Notice the response of the sheep, "Lord, when did we see you hungry and feed you?" (25:37). The righteous sheep had been so transformed into Christ-likeness that "loving their neighbors as themselves" had become an act of mercy to them. It had become a part of their spiritual DNA, so to speak. Their response warrants their reward.

The goats, however, didn't take care of those in need and love their neighbors. They were surprised because they didn't see Jesus, and then didn't know how they could have helped him if they didn't have the chance. And so our text takes us back to Matt. 22:37–40, when Jesus explained the greatest two commandments: loving God and loving your neighbor. You may not realize that you love God when you love your neighbor, but you are. Of course, the goats were confused because they never saw Jesus in person, and therefore they thought they didn't have an opportunity to help Jesus. I often imagine them giving further reply by saying, "But Jesus, we never saw you! We only saw the tax collectors, prostitutes, a stranger on the other side of the road, who we were careful to walk around, and sinners . . . but we never saw you!" It is in this final judgment that we see this truth: When you love your neighbor, you love God.

It's hard to miss the connection with the poor performance of the Temple by not caring for people other than themselves with the encouragement to the disciples to be ready by being prepared and loving their neighbors. There is a strong contrast here that can easily be overlooked if we simply look at these passages individually and take them out of the greater context of the ongoing dialogue with Jesus and the teachers of the law, which Matthew has created. Because of this context into which the parable of the sheep and goats are imbedded, we must be careful not to assume that this parable of judgment is trying to tell us that the way to get into heaven is based on works. Indeed, one can only be granted eternal life by having faith in Jesus Christ and by accepting God's grace. It then should become an obedient response to love God and love your neighbor.

BE READY

As I learned in my early years of being a Christian, looking for signs will never fulfill the desire or requirement to "be ready." I believe the appointed time has been hidden from us because if we knew the day and the hour, then almost everyone would be found ready—but probably for the wrong reasons. This necessarily wouldn't be a bad thing if the power of Christianity is found in eternal rewards and investments. However, the real power of Christianity is found in the restoration of broken people. By the life, death, and resurrection of Jesus, those who are broken can be made whole again. Transformation is a part of the process; Jesus desires to renew us day by day. God's mission in the world is to bring restoration—holistic restoration spiritually, physically, and in other ways. The sheep in the parable were so transformed to love their neighbor as themselves that they didn't realize they were, in effect, taking care of Jesus. They didn't see him because they "saw" him often. Conversely, the goats missed out on many opportunities presented to them. Just like the religious leaders in the parable of the Good Samaritan (Luke 10:25–37), they didn't recognize Jesus because they failed to see him in the people around them. They didn't take care of the people close to God's heart.

Apocalyptic spirituality motivates us to be ready when the Master returns for his servants and to establish fully his Kingdom. Do you truly want to "be ready" for the return of Jesus? Please know that it doesn't matter how well you know the signs and try to predict when he is returning. You can still be shut out from the banquet because you are not ready spiritually. When that Day of Judgment comes, the church will be saved by the grace of God, judged by their declaration of Jesus as the Son of God. However, we can't ignore Jesus' concern for loving our neighbors. Loving our neighbors is a fruit of loving God.

4

Paul's Apocalyptic Shadow

But our citizenship is in heaven. And we eagerly await
a Savior from there, the Lord Jesus Christ, who, by the
power that enables him to bring everything under his
control, will transform our lowly bodies so that they will
be like his glorious body.

—Phil. 3:20–21

THE APOSTLE PAUL SPENT much of his energy trying to prepare
the church for the Lord's return in the beginning years of church
history. He even advised the Corinthian church in his first letter,
as we shall soon see, not to worry about getting married because
the Lord was returning soon, and they must do the work of the
gospel to prepare for the Kingdom of God. He did, however, allow marriage when a person burned with passion, and therefore
recommended it as an escape from sexual sin. Even with the allowance for marriage, Paul was chiefly concerned with the church's
spiritual formation. The return of the Lord was so imminent to
Paul that much of his teaching was influenced by this overarching
concern that he might simply run out of time before Jesus' second
coming. This immanence hung over the early church like a thick

fog as it cast an apocalyptic shadow of influence on Paul's ministry. Edith M. Humphrey says the following about Paul's apocalyptic shadow:

> Paul himself writes no full-blown apocalypse. Yet 2 Corinthians, along with his other letters, displays a complete familiarity with the apocalyptic tradition, while using its themes, forms, and ideas in ways that surprise the reader. Paul in fact reconfigured apocalyptic discourse itself, in the light of his own conviction that the "future intervening judgment and salvation" and the "impinging reality of another world" had in a definitive sense already occurred in the person of Jesus Christ through the Spirit. The future dimension, of course, is not wholly subsumed, as Paul anticipates the fulfillment of what has begun, in the life of the church and the world as a whole. Paul's rhetoric is of necessity subtle, since it is governed as much by his reserve toward things normally construed as apocalyptic as it is by his acceptance and experience of them.[1]

Paul's writings may not be considered apocalyptic literature, and some Christians reject any apocalypticism in Paul. But we can't ignore the apocalyptic influence that overshadows much of his thinking and practical theology—an influence found in multiple places throughout the New Testament.

DEEP SPIRITUAL FORMATION

In light of Paul's apocalyptic shadow, he wasn't concerned about or preaching about an escapism theology that tries superficially to "save" as many people as possible. Paul's ministry and energies were spent on creating deep people for Jesus Christ. He wanted to help people experience the grace of God and experience deep, restorative spiritual formation. Paul's instructions for practical living were based on his deep desire to help the young church

1. Humphrey, "Ambivalent Apocalypse: Apocalyptic Rhetoric and Intertextuality in 2 Corinthians," in *The Intertexture of Apocalyptic Discourse in the New Testament*, 114.

be spiritually transformed into the likeness of Jesus Christ. Even though some of Paul's practical applications for living in an apocalyptic shadow were suited for short-term application, his theology and spiritual formation have timeless relevance. Paul's emphasis on deep transformational spiritual formation rang harmoniously with Jesus' apocalyptic spirituality, which also emphasized the transformation of the person's soul. It was this internal transformation by the grace of God that made a person righteous and worthy of eternal life. It was under this great apocalyptic shadow that the early church was conceived and developed.

Paul and the early church probably expected that the Lord would return in their lifetimes. However, we can imagine their dilemma when they began to die and the Lord still hadn't returned. Paul had to address very practical concerns that arose under this apocalyptic shadow. In 1 Cor. 15:51, he spoke to this "mystery" and made mention that "not all will sleep." Sleeping in this context was a metaphor for death. Also, his discourse on the resurrection in 1 Cor. 15 was developed primarily because people in the church were dying, and those left behind wondered what had happened to them since the Lord had not yet returned.

Paul's apocalyptic gospel also focused on God's coming judgment. Judaism, which was the vessel of religion for the Kingdom of God up until the arrival of Jesus Christ, had just been given several additional elements. These elements include the life, death, resurrection, and return of Jesus Christ to rule over the nations. Paul's gospel was concerned with teaching the first three and preparing the church for the last element, the reign of Christ, which included judgment. It was in this apocalyptic understanding that Paul was concerned about the church's spiritual formation. He was concerned about the hearts and righteousness of the people of God and how they would be found on the Day of Judgment.

RUN THE RACE

While attending high school in Marion, Indiana, I was a sprinter on the track team and ran the grueling 110 high hurdles as well as the

300 meter low hurdles. In the beginning of the season, I ran a race, and I thought I had won—I'm still convinced that I did! However, it was determined that the runner just behind me in the next lane dove forward and threw his hand forward to cross the finish line just before I did. I was disappointed, but I had learned my lesson. Toward the end of the same season, I had the chance to apply what I'd learned from that season opener. Our team was competing in a meet that would determine the county championship, and I was running the 110 high hurdles. Near the end of the race I came to the last few hurdles and trailed by one or two steps. I remembered what happened to me in the season opener and knew what I had to do. I pushed as hard as I could and aggressively sprinted the last few yards. As I approached the finish line I dove forward so hard that I lost control and went into a summersault crossing the line. While picking myself up from the pavement and trying to catch my breath, the runner who just seconds before was ahead of me was cheering and clearly believed that he had beaten me. However, when the timekeeper came and gave us our times, he told me that I had come in first. I was the county champion!

In several of his letters, Paul likened the Christian life to a runner competing to win a race and used terms like "strain toward what is ahead" and "press on toward the goal to win the prize" (Phil. 3:13–14). His audience in Philippi was well aware of these analogies since they lived in Greece, the birthplace of the Olympic Games.

Today when I read Paul's encouragement in 1 Cor. 9:24 to "run in such a way as to get the prize," I remember the medal I won for winning the county championship in high school and the effort and discipline it took to win it. You see, you can't win first place if you aren't running very hard. You also can't win a race without lots of training and practice. The apostle Paul, however, wasn't telling his readers to run a physical race, but to run a spiritual race—by the grace of God—using the same type of discipline and fortitude. His goal was for them to be spiritually formed into the full likeness of Christ Jesus, for which he took hold of us. Paul claimed that he hadn't gotten there yet, but in his letters, you can imagine him running as hard as he could and then somersaulting across the finish line!

Paul's encouragement to run a strong race of spiritual formation becomes even more interesting when you consider the apocalyptic shadow they lived under—namely the belief that Jesus could be coming back at any possible moment. Paul spent his time transforming himself and others through the presence and power of the Holy Spirit, into the likeness of Christ Jesus. He didn't spend his time deciphering the "signs" and telling people to meet him on a hill at a certain time on a certain day. He told people, "Hey, Jesus is coming soon. We need to be ready SPIRITUALLY so that when he comes, we can be found righteous." Paul's apocalyptic spirituality was focused on the transformational power of the gospel of Jesus Christ. The impending return of Jesus was extra motivation to be found ready spiritually so that, when Jesus returned like a thief in the night, Paul would be found diving across the finish line with his arms outstretched because he was pressing toward the prize so hard. Paul's focus under the apocalyptic shadow was the spiritual formation of the church and his own spirit.

APOCALYPTIC MARRIAGE

It's hard to imagine the pressures the early church faced in those beginning years. While we, the twenty-first-century church, struggle with the disregard of Christ's return over two thousand years after his ascension, Paul and the apostles lived in the immediacy of the New Testament events. I don't believe any of them thought it would take over two thousand years for Christ to return. However, that is where we find ourselves today. When we read the New Testament books, we must keep this apocalyptic timeline of the early church in mind.

For example, Paul's teaching on marriage in 1 Cor. 7 has been widely abused and largely taken out of the apocalyptic context. Some believe Paul was so dedicated to the call of the ministry that he thought marriage was a distraction and not worth the time. This passage comes after a lengthy teaching on how the marriage relationship should look and when marriage should occur. Paul seems to have a bias for staying unwed so that a person could focus on the work God has given the person. However, there is an allowance for marriage if you are burning with passion for a person of the opposite sex. After all, Paul says, "It is better to marry than to burn with passion" (1 Cor. 7:9). If this was Paul's long-life philosophy of marriage, what a negative and depressing ethic this would be! However, I believe there is another factor at play regarding Paul's motivation for singleness. For instance, take a look at 1 Cor. 7:29, "What I mean, brothers, is that the time is short. From now on those who have wives should live as if they had none; those who mourn, as if they did not; those who are happy, as if they were not; those who buy something, as if it were not theirs to keep; those who use the things of the world, as if not engrossed in them. For this world in its present form is passing away" (1 Cor. 7:29–31). This text highlights that Paul believed the return of Christ was so near that a person should live as if Jesus were returning tomorrow. Frederick Murphy stated it this way, "The world is rapidly coming to an end, and the best way for believers to spend their time is to get ready for the end."[2] Stop for a moment and imagine actually living this way. I'm fairly certain most Christian therapists would say that these are very unhealthy ways of living long term and would strongly encourage us to change our course of action.

It is good to understand the apocalyptic context in which Paul wrote. But understanding the context does not mean that Paul's end of the world teachings are irrelevant for our context today. We need to use discernment in understanding and applying Paul's teachings, including those about spiritual formation and holistic restoration.

If Paul understood that Jesus wasn't coming back for another two thousand plus years, then perhaps he wouldn't have encouraged people to remain single. He may have even felt led to develop a long-term perspective of marriage that helped people to use marriage to grow deeper in Christ. Either way, Paul's goal was

2. Murphy, *Apocalypticism in the Bible and Its World: A Comprehensive Introduction*, 347.

to spiritually develop the church as much as possible given the possible time frame he had. The point I'm making is that given a very short time frame and the goal of spiritually forming people as much as possible before the return of Christ, the items listed in verses 27–31 make more sense in a culture that believed that Jesus was coming back at any moment. However, Christ Jesus didn't return during the days of Paul, and we are still waiting today. Yet, Paul made every effort to challenge the young church to put all work into preparing themselves spiritually for the return of Christ Jesus.

PAULINE APOCALYPTIC SPIRITUALITY

With these passages in mind, we could learn a lot from Paul on how to live day-to-day as we anticipate the return of Christ Jesus. Perhaps some of us have spent too much time looking for signs and not enough time allowing God's grace to transform our spirits into the likeness of Christ. It is possible that some will be transformed very little into the likeness of Christ Jesus because they spend too much of their time looking for the signs of His coming. But, all whom are transformed by the grace of God won't be found sleeping when the thief comes.

So, that was then, and this is now. For two thousand years, the church has lived in Paul's apocalyptic shadow and his teaching of the imminent return of Christ. Throughout history, predictions of Christ's return to bring judgment and retribution have been made and then proven false. More recently, we've heard pronouncements of prophetic apocalypses from people like Harold Camping, the former president of Family Radio, a California based radio network, and other people based on the abrupt end to the Mayan calendar. During those times, even Christians were confused and sought direction on how to respond. To counter those and other false beliefs, we must look at Paul's spiritual formation theology in light of his understanding of impending apocalypse. We can then use this information as a resource to teach twenty-first-century Christians how to live in our modern apocalyptic times.

In the same way that Paul's impending apocalyptic shadow shaped and formed much of his theology, our current understanding of the Lord's return affects how we teach and communicate spiritual formation today. Since the beginning, the study of the end of the world has affected the church's view of spiritual formation and discipleship. Therefore, Revelation should not be interpreted lightly because it has cost innocent people their very lives and can shape the future of the church. Paul's influence and spiritual formation for the early church was done with a sense of an impending apocalypse. Yet despite his understanding that Jesus would return at any moment, Paul's plan on spiritual formation was focused on people becoming more and more like Christ rather than gathering the people together and simply waiting for Him to return. We can take comfort, knowing that no matter how dire things may seem or how imminent His return could be, we can focus our lives on the process of becoming more Christ-like and be ready for his return.

5

The Influences of Apocalyptic Spirituality on the Church and Society

"Look, he is coming with the clouds," and "every eye will
see him, even those who pierced him"; and all peoples on
earth "will mourn because of him." So shall it be! Amen.

—Rev. 1:7

AS WE HAVE BEEN discussing how apocalyptic spirituality affects
our personal spiritual formation, I also believe that apocalyptic
spirituality affects the cultural dynamics in which the church resides. Christian spirituality is lived out in local communities and
throughout society. This can be a very positive experience if the
apocalyptic spirituality is healthy and encourages a church community to strive to be more holistically Christ-like as it waits for
the return of Jesus Christ (just like Jesus and Paul exemplified for
us in chapters 3 and 4). However, if the spiritual formation is bent
more toward interpreting the signs of Christ's return and trying to
fulfill those physical signs here on earth, then apocalyptic spirituality can negatively affect communities and society. We see the

extreme cases of negative apocalyptic spirituality and its effects on a Christian community in cults that pop up with a cyclical frequency that remind us of how far these extreme interpretations can take us. For example, on April 10, 1993, seventy-six Students of the Seven Seals led by David Koresh died in a fire deliberately set by the leadership from a distorted view of how the end times would occur. They greatly affected their local communities and left a global trail of pain and bewilderment for those who were connected with their misguided views of apocalyptic spirituality. I understood that day, as I watched the situation in Waco, Texas unfold before my eyes, that people's understanding of the end of the world could have serious consequences for their lives today.

This chapter is not meant simply to entertain you, the reader, in a sensational way with extreme cases of apocalyptic spirituality as if this were an "Apocalyptic Spirituality Gone Wild" video. Rather, the reason I present these cases in history is to remind the church of the responsibility it has to understand rightly apocalyptic spirituality. Its purpose is to help people "be ready" in a spiritually formative way, rather than let our brothers and sisters get swept away with an understanding that is simply more entertaining than restorative.

I would also like to say that this chapter is not meant to be an exhaustive study on the historical influences of apocalyptic spirituality. For a more in depth understanding of how apocalyptic spirituality influences America's history, see Paul Boyer's book, *When Time Shall Be No More.*[1] Another great resource is a movie by PBS entitled, *APOCALYPSE!*[2] *These sources give insight and an accurate timeline to introduce to you some of the historical influences of Revelation and apocalyptic spirituality on world cultures.*

1. Boyer, *When Time Shall Be No More: Prophecy Belief in Modern American Culture.*

2. Cran and Loeterman. *Apocalypse!: The Story of the Book of Revelation,* VHS. FRONTLINE, 1999.

EARLY CHURCH

Since the early days of Christianity, persecution and martyrdom have been the repeated consequence of claiming Christ Jesus as Lord and Savior, beginning with Stephen in the first century to the untold thousands imprisoned and killed for their faith in the world today. Persecution is a characteristic of the faith because, as Peter said, we simply don't belong in this world (1 Pet. 2:10–12). We are aliens and strangers. This is largely why I believe that Revelation was written and given to the church. It reminds us that this world is ultimately not our home and we are simply "passing through," even though Christians believe that they should pass through the world justly and compassionately.

Stephen was the first Christian martyr. He stood before the Sanhedrin and proclaimed Jesus to be the Messiah and Son of God, and it cost him his life. Countless other Christians would join him in the next few centuries who were persecuted not only by Rome for not declaring Caesar as a god (little g), but also by the Jews because Christians were charged with worshiping too many God's (big G). There are ancient accounts of Christians, including Ignatius (a student of John the Apostle), who were thrown into the coliseum for sport and torn to pieces by wild animals. Tacitus in his work *Annals* described some of these tortures:

> And so, to get rid of this rumor, Nero set up [i.e., falsely accused] as the culprits and punished with the utmost refinement of cruelty a class hated for their abominations, who are commonly called Christians. Christus, from whom their name is derived, was executed at the hands of the procurator Pontius Pilate in the reign of Tiberius. Checked for a moment, this pernicious superstition again broke out, not only in Judea, the source of the evil, but even in Rome. . ... Accordingly, arrest was first made of those who confessed [to being Christians]; then, on their evidence, an immense multitude was convicted, not so much on the charge of arson as because of [their] hatred for the human race. Besides being put to death they were made to serve as objects of amusement; they were clothed in the hides of beasts and torn to death by dogs;

others were crucified, others set on fire to serve to illuminate the night when daylight failed. Nero had thrown open his grounds for the display, and was putting on a show in the circus, where he mingled with the people in the dress of charioteer or drove about in his chariot. All this gave rise to a feeling of pity, even towards men whose guilt merited the most exemplary punishment; for it was felt that they were being destroyed not for the public good but to gratify the cruelty of an individual.[3]

Those early Christians must have thought they were living the book of Revelation, which was written during their era and in their culture. Their apocalyptic spirituality was more akin to what Jesus and Paul taught: hang in there; the end is coming; therefore, finish the race strong, and hold to your faith as you become more and more like Jesus. They did not have to look for signs—the end of the world was upon them.

CONSTANTINE

In 313 CE, Constantine changed the game. Until then, the book of Revelation, which was not considered part of the canon of Scripture yet, had given insight to Christians that the end was indeed near, as various persecutions came and went over the first few hundred years of the church. Suddenly, by the decision of one man, Christianity was not only acceptable as a monotheistic religion that refused to accept Caesar as Lord, but it soon became the religion of the empire under Theodosius. Imagine the great paradigm shift that must have occurred in the minds of those early believers. They no longer had to hide their values and beliefs, but could openly express them—and even share them with others without fear of persecution.

Imagine what those people began to think about the message of Revelation? Suddenly, a book that was extremely relevant to their culture and circumstances regarding their suffering and tribulation had become almost obsolete. It was during this time

3. Tacitus, *Annals*, XV.44.

that the message of Revelation began to go into hibernation. Without active persecution, the church may not have known what to do
with it. Later, it is believed that Augustine, an early fifth century
leader in the church, helped recognize the book of Revelation as
part of the official New Testament canon at the Council of Car-
thage. Augustine supported an allegorical interpretation and even
expressed this viewpoint in his work, *City of God,* when the Roman Empire fell to the Goths.[4]

THE CRUSADES

In 1095, Pope Urban II proclaimed the First Crusade at the Council of Claremont with the goal of "taking back" Jerusalem and the
Holy Lands from the Muslims. The Crusades were very compli-
cated events that involved religion, politics, power, and geography,
and we cannot talk about them only as wars that were instigated
from a skewed understanding of the significance of the Holy Lands
in end time events. However, Pope Urban II exaggerated the anti-
Christian acts of the Muslim to rally people to fight in the Crusades. Pope Urban II went as far as to promise all who died in the
service of Christ, absolution and remission of sins to the countless
Christian warriors. Many of them fought and died in a war against
trained soldiers believing that they would be granted eternal life
because of their efforts. Apocalyptic spirituality helped to rally the
Christian warriors to fight for the land owners who may only have
wished to increase their lands and riches. There surely was a sense
that this battle could be the very Armageddon talked about in the
book of Revelation.

Even in many of today's end time prophecies, the Holy Land
plays a central role in the understanding of how the world will
come to an end. Unfortunately, as it was during the Crusades,
human lives can be considered by some to be secondary to the
fulfillment of apocalyptic signs. People are willing to count numerous casualties a necessity to fulfilling what they believe to be

4. Augustine of Hippo, *City of God.*

the end of the world and the beginning of the second coming of Jesus. However, if their understanding is wrong, then how can we justify allowing the violence to continue based upon apocalyptic speculation?

CHRISTOPHER COLUMBUS

American children often grow up learning the famous rhyme by Jean Marzollo that helps them remember Christopher Columbus's great achievement: *In 1492, Columbus sailed the ocean blue.* We are taught about his courageous sense of adventure as an explorer, and we even celebrate him on a national holiday. However, we rarely hear the back story that Christopher Columbus actually sailed the "ocean blue" with the purpose of discovering an alternate route to the orient to help reclaim Jerusalem from the Muslims and begin fulfilling the prophecies of the last days.[5] He was not expecting to find a new world when he landed in what is believed to be Central America. In his later years, Columbus wrote that even though he didn't find the back door to the Orient, perhaps the New World would supply the wealth required to finance a war to take back the Holy Lands. If Christopher Columbus did not believe in the need to take back the Holy Land for apocalyptic purposes, then perhaps our history would have been written much differently.

THOMAS MÜNTZER

In 1525, Thomas Müntzer, an early Reformation-era German theologian and pastor, became involved in the Peasant's Revolt (1524–25). He was a fiery and apocalyptic preacher, caught up in watching for signs preceding the end of the age, and interpreted the conflict between the common people and German nobility as the great battle discussed in the book of Revelation. He exhibited little concern for the economic oppression of the peasants but joined their cause to rally them for what he thought would be the

5. Delaney, *Columbus and the Quest for Jerusalem.*

final apocalyptic battle to usher in the return of Jesus. Paul Boyer describes it this way:

> As a coalition of German princes mobilized against the rebels, Müntzer invoked the language of biblical apocalypse to justify the peasants' cause. As the decisive battle took shape near Frankenhausen, he roused the ill-equipped rebels with a speech full of eschatological allusions. With God's help, he allegedly assured them, he himself would catch the cannonballs in his shirtsleeves. As the peasants sang hymns and looked for Christ's return to support their cause, the attack began. An estimated five thousand rebels died in the resulting slaughter; Müntzer himself was beheaded on May 15, 1525.[6]

Müntzer is considered a hero and martyr to modern day Communists whose greatest achievement was to rouse the German peasants to fight for their economic and political rights. He is forever remembered in the largest oil painting in the world which covers 1,722 sq. meters: The Peasant's War Panorama, located in Bad Frankenhausen, Germany.[7] Yet I wonder: Would those rebels have been willing to go against such insurmountable odds if they weren't convinced that Jesus Himself was going to join them in battle and defeat the German nobility? We'll never know, and it dismays me to think of the disappointment and sense of betrayal they experienced in their final moments as they waited in vain for divine help to come.

PURITANS AND THE NEW WORLD

In 1620, Pilgrims began their journey aboard the Mayflower to North America to escape the persecution they experienced from

6. Boyer, *When Time Shall Be No More: Prophecy Belief in Modern American Culture*, 58.

7. The rotunda painting was commissioned by the Socialist Unity Party of Germany to Professor Werner Tübke. Professor Tübke completed the 404 ft. wide by 46 ft. high painting in 1987. The panorama was inaugurated by Kurt Hager and Morgot Honecker on September 14, 1989, eight weeks before the fall of the Berlin Wall.

the Church they wanted to reform in England. They traveled across the Atlantic Ocean with the hope of beginning a new colony in which they could have the freedom to own land and express their faith. Slowly, in present day Massachusetts, they began to colonize America in hopes of creating the New Jerusalem. I wonder how they could not have seen America as the New Jerusalem as they sought to escape persecution and begin building a new land. There are many similarities to the book of Revelation to which many of the Puritans could relate.

Ten years later, the Puritan lawyer John Winthrop helped found the Massachusetts Bay Colony. While leading a large group of people across the Atlantic to the New World, he gave a sermon on his ship the *Arabella* that said, in part,

> The eyes of the world will be upon us. We are as a city upon a hill, raised up. You may think we're in the howling wilderness. You may think we're out beyond the farthest beyond. But in fact, God's providence is such that as the latter days begin to unfold, this may indeed be the city, the New Jerusalem that's unfolding before not only our eyes but the eyes of the world.[8]

Winthrop's leadership and constant apocalyptic rhetoric helped shape the mindset of the colonials working to build a New Jerusalem. His apocalyptic rhetoric helped build their colony, and he even served as governor for twelve of the colony's first twenty years.

COTTON MATHER

One of the challenges of preaching an apocalyptic message is that sooner or later someone would dare to ask, "When will it happen?" And there have been many who actually attempted to answer this question. Cotton Mather (1663–1728), an influential Puritan minister whose writings and speeches played a large role in the Salem witch trials of 1692, was one of the first colonial Americans to answer this question. He told the people that the end would

8. Winthrop, "A City Upon a Hill": A Model of Christian Charity.

come in 1697. However, the year came and went, and the colonials found themselves still in America. So Mather went back to the Bible for more study and determined a new date, which was 1736. That date didn't seem to work for him, so later he moved it back to 1716. Once again, the year came and went with no apocalypse in sight. Naturally, his followers were frustrated because they had been living in anticipation of the Day of Judgment the entire year. Mather made several more predictions in the following years with the same result. Then in 1727, a large earthquake shook the Boston area, and Mather excitedly predicted that the end of the world had arrived. Unfortunately, it was the end . . . not for the world but for Cotton Mather. He died shortly after his final apocalyptic announcement. Since his death almost three hundred years ago, many others have tried and continue to try to answer the same question: "When will the end of the world come?"

THE AMERICAN REVOLUTION

Those looking back to consider the early days of our country, especially the first hundred years or so, have to understand the apocalyptic influence upon which the New World was built. And to that foundation was added a war with the British who were traditionally seen as the "oppressors." It's easy to imagine the apocalyptic imagery and anticipation that was in the minds of many. Then, in 1776, the American Revolution began because the colonists believed they were being taxed too heavily and unfairly because they had no voice in the British government. The Stamp Act, passed by the British parliament in 1765, was interpreted by many as the Mark of the Beast referred to in Rev. 13:16–18. Propaganda was also distributed at that time illustrating King George as the anti-Christ. All this has been said to underscore the point that, while the apocalyptic understanding of the colonists didn't directly lead to the American Revolution, it did much to create a form of validation in the minds of the religious for the actions they were about to take.

THE SHAKERS

In 1780, the United Society of Believers in Christ's Second Appearing, commonly known today as the Shakers were formed in England. A few years later, several Shaker families settled in the American colonies. They formed the Millennial Church, a corporate body they created to "live in community" as they waited for the Lord's return. Unfortunately, by 1820, most of the communities had died out because they believed in celibacy. Conversion was their only means of growth, and they most likely lived celibate lives due to Paul's apocalyptic teaching to the Corinthians (1 Cor. 7). Paul encouraged the believers in Corinth to remain unmarried to devote more time to their spiritual formation because "time was running out."

LATTER-DAY SAINTS

In 1830, as part of the Second Great Awakening, Joseph Smith set out to establish what he called the "New Jerusalem" in Independence, Missouri. Smith, who years earlier had started the Church of Jesus Christ of Latter-Day Saints, also known as Mormons, rallied people to his cause and began to build his kingdom and establish the New Jerusalem. His purpose was to create both religious and secular institutions in the New Jerusalem and create a seat of government that would rule the entire North and South American continents, to build a greater Kingdom of God. The Mormons continue to build the New Jerusalem today and, as of July, 2014, boast a little over fifteen million members worldwide.

SEVENTH DAY ADVENTISTS

Another group to be birthed out of the Second Great Awakening was the Seventh Day Adventists. William Miller, a Baptist minister and founder of the sect, believed that Jesus Christ would return in the year 1844. Samuel Snow, a disciple of Miller, took it one step farther and predicted that Jesus would return on October 22 of that year. The followers of William Miller's prediction became known as the Millerites. The movement began small but steadily grew to around 100,000 people who gathered from New York and Massachusetts. Millerites believed so strongly that Jesus would return on October 22nd that many of them sold all their possessions and gathered together as a community to wait for Jesus' arrival. Sadly, he never came, and that day became known in history as The Great Disappointment. One Millerite named Henry Emmons later reflected on the experience:

> I waited all Tuesday [October 22] and dear Jesus did not come—I waited all the forenoon of Wednesday, and was well in body as I ever was, but after 12 o'clock I began to feel faint, and before dark I needed someone to help me up to my chamber, as my natural strength was leaving me very fast, and I lay prostrate for 2 days without any pain—sick with disappointment.[9]

Miller continued to wait for Jesus in great anticipation until his death in 1849. His movement continued and is still in existence today. We know them as the Seventh Day Adventists, and they number roughly 17.5 million as of 2014. Although their belief in the imminent return of Jesus has lessened, the denominational apocalyptic stance has not, shown by the following statement:

> While Seventh-day Adventists arose within an apocalyptic movement that stressed the nearness of the Second Advent, their "Christian" heritage emphasized the down-to-earth implications of the ministry of the Saviour.[10]

So while the Seventh Day Adventists began institutionally from the Great Disappointment, today their focus is on the life and ministry of Jesus Christ.

---

9. Knight, *Millennial Fever: A Study of Millerite Adventism*, 217–18.

10. http://www.adventist.org/information/

JOHN DARBY AND CYRUS SCOFIELD

Another contributor to the apocalyptic sensationalism in the nineteenth century was John Nelson Darby. In the 1830s, Darby developed a new end-time understanding of the Scriptures that believed faithful Christians would be flown up to heaven before a great tribulation of suffering would overtake the earth. Today, this is known as the secret "rapture." Darby's creation of the rapture as a secret event was a new idea that has no predecessor in church history. However, the idea of Revelation being a map of history that is fulfilled through dispensations was not a new idea in light of church history. He believed the Bible, including the book of Revelation, was an outline of apocalyptic eras. These eras were then, and are today, known as "dispensations." Darby changed the game with his theory of the secret rapture because he didn't put a date on when it would happen. It's simply always around the corner. Darby's rapture theory was in line with what is known as pre-millennialism. Pre-millennialism is the belief that the world will get worse before the return of Jesus Christ, including periods of tribulation and divine wrath, before he will reign for one thousand years.

Cyrus Scofield (1843–1921) was an innovative pastor who paired Darby's work with the King James Bible. The Scofield Reference Bible was released in 1909, and soon it was the most influential statement of dispensational pre-millennialism. Scofield included Darby's commentary into the Bible by inserting his teaching into the margins. This technique was done only once before when the Geneva Bible was translated in 1560. Scofield's Reference Bible became very popular during World War I, because suddenly the idea of world peace and the concept of the world getting better and better didn't seem very realistic. The Reference Bible became amazingly popular because of its pre-millennial bent that the world would get worse before Jesus returned. Darby's pre-millennial dispensationalism has been popular ever since then and still increases in popularity whenever times of disaster or war appear on the horizon. However, this interpretation leaves little, if any, encouragement for spiritual formation from the book of Revelation today—we're simply to wait and watch for the signs of his appearing.

HAL LINDSEY

In 1970, Hal Lindsey published *The Late, Great Planet Earth,* which quickly became a best seller.[11] His pre-millennial interpretation of Revelation, paired with his application of the Cold War between the Soviet Union and the Western nations, caused a renewed expectation among believers that the end was very near. This expectation, in turn, created an obsession with knowing the signs related to the return of Christ and the end of the world. Like their earlier counterparts, millions of believers spent countless hours reading Scripture to interpret the signs that foretell the end of the world. Lindsey's book created a sensationalism that distracted many Christians from a spiritually formative understanding of Revelation.

LEFT BEHIND FICTION NOVELS

In similar fashion, Tim LeHaye and Jerry Jenkins wrote a fictional series of books that dramatized Darby's and Scofield's pre-millennial dispensationalism and the theory of the secret rapture. The books became wildly popular and were even considered an unofficial commentary on Revelation in some fundamentalist circles.

Years ago, I taught several lessons from the book of Revelation at one of the churches where I served as lead pastor. Throughout the series, several of the attendees referenced the *Left Behind* book series as an authoritative source. I saw firsthand the influence of the *Left Behind* series because it brought a very difficult apocalyptic book into a modern context. People could understand the meaning of Revelation in a way they had not before. However, I believe the book series is more about pre-millennial dispensationalism

11. Lindsey and Carlson, *The Late, Great Planet Earth.*

than about preparing people for the return of Jesus and hearing him say, "Well done!"

In November of 2006, Inspired Media Games released a Christian real-time strategy game entitled, *Left Behind: Eternal Forces*, based on the *Left Behind* series. The setting of the video game was in a post-rapture New York City. (Post-rapture means that Jesus had returned and secretly removed all Christians from the earth.) The object of the video game was to convert as many people as possible to Christianity to build your "spirit" as well as your "army" (also known in the game as the Tribulation Force). The opposing force is the Global Community (non-Christians). However, if they will not convert, then you are allowed to use violence and kill them.

So, on a basic level, it's a video game designed from a dispensational pre-millennial viewpoint, and this understanding gives validation for so-called believers (even though the true church has been removed from the earth) to kill non-Christians. Many parents who would never purchase violent video games for their children had less restraint about buying *Left Behind: Eternal Forces* for their children. It was marketed as a Christian video game and supported their understanding of the end of the world as well. The passive message of the video game also alluded to being ready for the end times by simply being converted while knowing and looking for informational signs. However, Jesus' real teachings on "being ready" are less superficial and vastly more concerned about the inner transformation of a person from the inside out: a transformation of the heart, which leads to an outer transformation that enables us to love our neighbors spiritually, socially, and justly.

WHAT HISTORY HAS TAUGHT US

When we as Christians are faced with the option of following a sensational understanding of the end times or putting our effort into a transformative apocalyptic spirituality that requires daily commitment on our part, sadly, the sensational understanding usually wins out because it's easier. It becomes a form of escapism which teaches that we don't have to work at being "ready" for Jesus' return. Instead, all we have to do is read the so-called signs or understand the four cycles of the blood moon to be ready for the Day of Judgment.[12] It will be a great tragedy on the Day of Judgment to see all the people who were convinced that little to no effort for spiritual transformation was required by them to become more like Jesus Christ. God's mission in the world isn't as a realtor that only desires to help people land in the right "house."

God's mission in the world is more akin to a renovator who desires to redeem and restore you into what he intended you to be and bring you back into relationship with him. No sensational signs are required.

Throughout the years, denominations and churches have been founded based on the imminent return of Jesus for His people to take them to heaven and leave this sinful world behind. With that perspective, there's reduced motivation for true earthly transformation if the church is waiting for that transformation to happen after they go into eternity. When the church begins to see God's plan for uniting both heaven and earth in a spiritually transformational way here and now, the Kingdom of God on earth is realized, salvation is imparted, disciples are made, and the world will experience holistic restoration.

12. Hagee, *Four Blood Moons: Something Is About to Change.*

6

Rethinking the End of the World

Therefore keep watch, because you do not know the day
or the hour.

—Matt. 25:13

SINCE THE ASCENSION OF Christ in the first century, every subsequent generation has been looking for him to return. Being one of those generations, we have to ask ourselves, "What if it's another two thousand years until he comes?" God doesn't want us to know the day or hour so that when Jesus does come in glory, he'll see us for who we really are. The parables in Matt. 24–25 explain this to us. Therefore, we must maintain a sense of ownership and responsibility while on this earth. If we live each day of our lives as if we won't be here tomorrow, then those who come after us could suffer from our lack of temporal responsibility. *Believe it or not, there is space in the Christian faith to live here as responsible stewards, as if the world will not end in our life time, yet live with excitement that he may return any day.* That is the space in which we need to live to be an effective Kingdom of God on earth. If we are constantly "standing at the door with our bags packed," then how is the world going to trust our hearts and motives to change the earth on which we all live? Perhaps, like the parable in Matt. 25:14–30, we need to consider our lives in this world like the "gold" the servants in the parable were entrusted to use and invest until their master returned. Will Jesus be frustrated because we, like the third servant, buried our treasure and just stood idly waiting for the master to walk in the door? Or will he find us faithful when he returns? We have work to do, so let's be the church and co-labor with God.

In the previous chapter, we saw, for good or bad, how influential apocalyptic spirituality has been upon Western culture, which emphasized speculation and waiting, rather than obedience and actively loving our neighbors. I believe there is a way to view the end of the world according to Revelation that will allow us to be faithful and obedient servants and will not require the church to neglect the current culture because they are waiting for the arrival of the end times.

HOW CHRISTIANS OUGHT TO VIEW THE END OF THE WORLD TODAY

N. T. Wright, a leading New Testament scholar and former Bishop of Durham, England, provides one of the best approaches to modern end times understandings in his book *Surprised by Hope: Rethinking Heaven, the Resurrection, and the Mission of the Church*.[1] In it, Wright breaks down much of the Western concept about heaven as an eternal home of fluffy clouds with angels serving us in an afterlife of personal comfort and replaces it with the biblical perspective of God's design to unite heaven and earth in a lasting embrace.

Wright's book is timely because the Western church has become fixated with the afterlife, and a driving question has become, "Will I go to heaven or hell?" Christians are fascinated with "what comes next"—both personally and for the church as a whole. Over the years, hundreds of charts and pictographs have been published to describe how and when the world will end, and depending on

1. Wright, *Surprised by Hope: Rethinking Heaven, the Resurrection, and the Mission of the Church*, 19.

the millennial viewpoint of the author, whether it will occur before, during, or after the return of Jesus Christ. As we saw in the last chapter, religious institutions, denominations, and churches have been founded based on different theological viewpoints regarding the imminent return of Jesus to remove His people from an evil, sin-sick world. That perspective, however, leaves Christians waiting for a spiritual transformation to occur after they cross into eternity rather than for true earthly spiritual transformation (individually and corporately) that can occur in the world today.

I believe, however, that when the church truly understands God's vision for uniting heaven and earth in a way that affects life here and now, the richness and depth of God's mission in the world will be experienced. The focus would no longer be on me and what I choose to do with my time until heaven, but about God's plan and how I can partner with him as he re-creates the world in beautiful restoration.[2]

I believe God's purpose in our lives is to become more like Jesus, not simply to get into heaven in our present, yet redeemed state. If this is true, then our understanding of the end of the world should not be perceived as just a road map to get us from here to there, but as a motivator for fostering spiritual formation that creates earthly people with Christ-like personalities, who thereby exhibit heaven here on earth. Conversely, our understanding of the last days should not be shelved because people in previous centuries misinterpreted or misused the message found in Revelation. Rather, Jesus' teachings to us through the apostle John should be reexamined and understood in ways that will spiritually transform people's lives.

A NEW MISSION FOR THE CHURCH

Leslie Newbigin wrote a book in 1995 that described the church as a "mission station."[3] What he meant was that the church had

2. Wright, *Surprised by Hope: Rethinking Heaven, the Resurrection, and the Mission of the Church*, 184.

3. Newbigin, *The Open Secret: An Introduction to the Theory of Mission*, 144.

become a centralized location for ministry, and the church had begun to expect people to come to them to do ministry. However, after spending many years as a missionary, Newbigin argued that church shouldn't wait on people to come to them, but that the church should "go out" to the world as a missionary would do. Newbigin's writing had an influence on the modern day church and encouraged Christians to look outside the walls to see what God is doing.

This perspective of the church on a mission that's taking place in many Western churches has deep roots in a healthy understanding of the events leading up to the end of the world. For example, the emphasis on social and environmental justice is important because it's based on a belief that the world will be transformed and made new, not simply discarded when Jesus comes to "pick us up." However, it's a transformation for which God has chosen to include us. We have been chosen to co-labor with God in the great transformation of the world—the great restoration of the world to God's intended purposes. Somewhere in the story of God's mission in the world, we have forgotten the beginning and ending. Gabe Lyons, the founder of Q Ideas, a learning community that mobilizes Christians to advance the common good in society, describes it this way:

> The truncated Gospel that is often recounted is faithful to the fall and redemption pieces of the story, but largely ignores the creation and restoration components. These missing elements are at the heart of what a new generation of Christians are relearning, and subsequently, retelling.[4]

God's great "happily ever after" in Revelation involves the tree of life and his restored creation, new heaven and a new earth (including humanity), walking in his presence (Rev. 21:22–27). Few pastors today preach about the end of the world, and when they do, it's often detached from other spiritually formative teachings. They may excel when preaching about the fall and redemption,

4. Lyons, *The Next Christians: The Good News About the End of Christian America*, 51.

but they are unsure when preaching about the end of the world and the restoration of all creation. Consequently, they leave out two very important parts of God's eternal work: His creation at the beginning, and His work of earthly redemption in Rev. 21–22. The mission-minded perspective seeks to redeem the Gospel story and tell it all from beginning to end, from creation to the final restoration of all things. The church, especially the Western church, needs to experience a renewed understanding of the end times that enriches and explains God's true mission in the world today.

Understanding God's ultimate vision for this world plays a crucial role in understanding His current mission, because the entire New Testament has an underlying influence of apocalyptic spirituality. Fortunately, this context, like Paul's apocalyptic shadow, has been rediscovered within the past two centuries as Bible scholars revitalized the importance of Jewish historical-cultural background.[5]

Albert Schweitzer (1875–1965) was one of the first early twentieth century scholars to re-evaluate seriously how the Jewish understanding of the last days expressed itself in first century Jewish culture.[6] During his exploration for the historical Jesus, Schweitzer realized he couldn't fully understand the man without understanding the culture in which he lived. And central to the Jewish culture at that time was the apocalyptic expectation of a coming messiah. Although Schweitzer erroneously concluded that the real Jesus was just a man and not the divine Son of God Christians worship, he did much to raise awareness about an important point neglected for centuries, namely, that a contextual understanding of Jewish tradition and apocalyptic spirituality is crucial to understanding and interpreting the New Testament. It is possible to appreciate the social and religious context of Jesus' life and ministry without rejecting the supernatural core of the gospel.

The previous chapter gave several examples of how one's understanding of end time events can shape their spiritual formation

---

5. Boston Collaborative Encyclopedia of Western Theology, "On Albert Schweitzer," http://www.csus.edu/indiv/c/craftg/Hist127/Schweitzerideas.pdf
6. Ibid.

and world view—and then, for good or bad, affect everyone around them. With this in mind, isn't it both logical and ethical to apply a correct understanding of the last days when developing and teaching spiritually formative programs? If we take the Great Commission found in Matthew 28 seriously and truly believe that making disciples is a top priority, then the church must develop programs to promote a healthy spiritual formation based on a restorative understanding of the apocalyptic messages found in Scripture.

The "truncated gospel," referred to earlier in a quote by Gabe Lyons, states that while the church has been faithful in telling the story of the fall and redemption, it has neglected the important themes in apocalypticism: creation and restoration. The emphasis on creation was lost somewhere in church history, while the emphasis on restoration was replaced by the more current theology of evacuation, like the secret rapture, for example. A healthy biblical understanding of God's mission in the world begins "In the beginning God created the heavens and the earth," and concludes with His final restoration of all things, including the earth.

RECLAIMING THE BEGINNING AND THE END

One of the challenges of having an eschatology that focuses on escapism is that you tend to value the things in this life less or, at the very least, don't value some things as worth your time. For example, imagine that your house is on fire. The primary concern is the safety of you and anyone else in the house, so you grab all those living there and flee. The house may have burned down, but that doesn't matter because you have your life and your love ones around you. When a person believes that the world is going to be annihilated and we are waiting for a secret rapture to occur to rescue us from the burning world, we tend not to value the things in the world very much because "it's all going to burn anyway." Therefore, long term projects are often discouraged because we need to "get everyone out of the house." This is why long term social and environmental justice ministries were disparaged by the church for so long. More and more churches are seeing value in this world and are deciding to step up and "invest" in the world because God has plans to restore his creation.

Unfortunately, there are still many evangelical churches today that have little interest in efforts to restore social and environmental injustices and don't believe it to be a part of God's mission. The secular press even took note of it. The December 30, 2010 edition of the *New York Times* contained an article reporting on the evangelical backlash to creation care; that is, care for God's good creation. In the article, some Christians went as far as to label concern for the environment as "The Green Dragon."[7] Those churches hold to an understanding of the last days that does not involve God re-creating the world, but rather His wiping the slate clean so He can start over. To them, the spending of time and resources to help transform the world socially and environmentally is a distraction from the church's true agenda of spreading the gospel of Jesus Christ. By labeling a concern for the environment as the Green Dragon, Christians interviewed for the *Times* article labeled concern for creation as an anti-Christ that seeks to destroy the church.

Instead of viewing creation concern as anti-church and anti-Christ, imagine a healthy biblical understanding of the end of the world that believes God's plan is to restore and re-create the earth as well as believers. This understanding seeks to:

- Bring people into a personal relationship with Jesus Christ,

- Create mature Christians by developing them into the likeness of Jesus, and

- Value the earth as a creation of the Creator.

Those who adhere to these end time views would ultimately promote justice and compassion for the oppressed because they would co-labor with God to eradicate injustice and the suffering that comes with it. A restorative perspective of the last days would value spiritual, social, and environmental concerns because God

7. Rudolf, "An Evangelical Backlash against Evironmentalism," http://green.blogs.nytimes.com/2010/12/30/an-evangelical-backlash-against-environmentalism/

created this world for us to live in, and he is vitally interested in these areas as well. Rather than preparing for "someday," a restorative understanding seeks to live out the holistic mission of God for the world today. This means sharing the gospel in a context that also promotes social and environmental justice. Fortunately, organizations that practice this type of healthy, restorative last day perspective actually exist and are making an impact on the world.

One such organization is Eden Reforestation Projects, founded in 2001 by Steve Fitch and headquartered in Glendora, California. Its purpose is to alleviate extreme poverty through environmental stewardship by providing employment to local village workers to plant trees—millions and millions of trees—in Ethiopia, Madagascar, Nepal, and Haiti. I have personally traveled to Ethiopia several times and witnessed the transformation and restoration that this non-profit organization has done for the Kingdom of God and the Ethiopian people. Led by Fitch, Eden Reforestation Projects has given hope to thousands of people living in the devastated environment of central Ethiopia. To date, Eden Reforestation Projects has planted over ninety million trees, but that number increases by another two million every month. In conjunction with the tree planting is the creation of over three quarters of a million workdays for unemployed people and the rebuilding of communities along with environmental prosperity. Fitch's vision for Eden Reforestation Projects comes from an end of the world perspective that believes two things: God has a plan to re-create the world and free it from the bondage of sin, and His people are invited to partake in that task with Him.

Hope Dies Last is a social justice organization in Eastern Europe that counteracts human trafficking. They seek long-term ministry with those who are caught in the sex industry. This ministry is more complex than simply rescuing the victims from a physical threat. Sex trafficking is a very dehumanizing form of injustice that leads the victims to doubt their worth. Even if you are able to rescue someone from the physical threat of human trafficking, you can't guarantee that they won't return because the injustice is also spiritual and psychological. Hope Dies Last realizes this and has created a long-term ministry to reach women and men trapped in sexual exploitation and human trafficking. By reaching people with the gospel, people are empowered to make their own future choices, enabling Hope Dies Last to come alongside them. This way, the victims are empowered to leave the bondage of slavery when they are ready. This not only has a higher chance of counteracting the human trafficking effort, but it also heals and restores the whole person. A ministry like this involves patience and a perspective that isn't sitting around waiting for the end of the world to come sooner so that human trafficking will cease, but it involves a passion to roll up the sleeves and get involved in this world *while* we wait for Jesus' return.

A restorative understanding of the end times is not necessarily a new perspective in the history of understanding Revelation. In many ways, it is similar to the mission-minded church in that it seeks to re-emphasize an important element to the book of Revelation: justice and restoration. Many modern interpretations that aren't experiencing persecution have created elaborate end time theories to make Revelation relevant to our culture. One popular example of this is the *Left Behind* series discussed in chapter 5. The premise of the books is to create a global, political situation in which Revelation suddenly becomes relevant. However, this perspective is very American because we have many Christians around the world who are currently experiencing trials and tribulations without having to create apocalyptic scenarios.

However, if we were to take the book of Revelation into the Middle East, the book would carry much more relevance for the Christians who are dying for their faith. They don't need to "wait" for their persecution and tribulation. They are living in its shadow daily.

A restorative understanding of Revelation has not been the popular historical understanding of future events in Western culture as we saw in the last chapter. A restorative understanding of Revelation is crucial for understanding God's mission in the world. This is very important because how the church views the ultimate fate of the world and how it perceives God's current activity in the world directly affect its understanding of individual and corporate spiritual formation.

The Western church has shied away from these kinds of interpretation and practical application of apocalyptic literature because of the confusing imagery and contexts found in books like Daniel and Revelation. But, if the church is truly to understand God's mission in the world from His perspective, then it must adapt a healthier understanding of the last days. Empowered with this restorative perspective, the church may move forward in its mission to counteract environmental and social injustices with confidence as it practices the holistic gospel of Jesus.

7

The Forgotten Paradise

The Lord God took the man and put him in the Garden
of Eden to work it and take care of it.

—Gen. 2:15

IN 2014, THE BARNA Group, a Christian research company located
in Southern California, published a study revealing that only 19%
of Christians polled read their Bible four times or more a week.[1]
With such a small percentage of believers actively engaged in the
Bible, how can the church develop a healthy understanding of
God's plan for the world? One of the responsibilities I have on staff
at The Flipside Church is to teach a class titled "How to Study the
Bible," and I love it! It energizes me! One of the lessons I teach during the class is how to properly "observe" the Bible when we read it.
Oftentimes, when we read the Bible, we merely see the words and
stories we read but don't actively observe them. Let me give you an
example. If you attend your church regularly, then you have un-
doubtedly seen your sanctuary many times. I wonder, then, if you
know how many seats are in it. What is the distance from the front

1. https://www.barna.org/barna-update/culture/664-the-state-of-the-
bible-6-trends-for-2014#.VODLMvnF9h4

entrance to the stage? How many Bibles are available for attendees to use during the services? Although you see all these things on a regular basis, you may not have taken the time to *observe* the details and know the answers to these questions. In the same way, we are good at seeing the words in the Bible, but most of us haven't taken the time to dig in and observe what the Bible is trying to communicate to us on a deeper level. In light of the Barna Group study that was previously mentioned, my question and concern is: If only 19 percent of Christians are reading and seeing the Bible on a regular basis, then how many Christians are studying and *observing* the Bible more deeply? My educated guess is that about 5 to 7 percent of Christians are digging into the word of God and studying who God is and what his mission is in the world today. Unfortunately, I fear that even this number may be a bit optimistic.

When we simply read the Bible and don't look deeper to observe it, our brain allows our presuppositions, our own experiences, and other cultural influences to fill the information gaps. Let's look at how this phenomenon works by considering the topic of heaven, a subject that we tend to allow culture and experience to define.

When we take the time to study what the Bible says about heaven, we find that it projects a much different picture than what many Christians believe: a place devoid of work—even a very boring place! They imagine heaven as a place where we simply sit around chatting. There may be a few angels hanging out nearby strumming harps. This image is light years away from the picture of heaven that the Bible communicates to us. Many people, Christians and non-Christians alike, don't understand this because they simply don't take the time to observe what the Bible says about heaven and why we will be there.

When you go to the creation story in the book of Genesis and read about the creation of the Garden of Eden and the first people, you will notice that creation seems to be just as important as humanity (Gen. 2:4–25). Adam is, in fact, literally created from the dust of the earth (2:7). There is a co-dependent relationship where the land cannot thrive without the care of man, and man cannot survive without the land. You will also notice that God made man and placed him in the Garden of Eden to *work* the land and care for it (2:15). Just as God works, he wants humanity to work as well. So we see from the very beginning, even before the fall of Adam and Eve, that people were created to be busy, to work. This work was good and fulfilling to humanity and pleasing to God. However, when sin entered the picture, the fall caused work to become difficult and toilsome (3:17–19).

Now, have you ever stopped to think that perhaps we will have work to do in heaven? If work and creation are so intimately entwined and God is actively working to restore creation at the end of all things, then would it also be logical to conclude that we will have work to do in heaven? I believe so. There are allusions to heaven throughout the Old and New Testaments that include, or at least hint, to the concept of work. Isa. 2:4 is a famous passage that speaks to the eternal peace that we will share in heaven. It says, "He will judge between the nations and will settle disputes for many peoples. They will beat their swords into plowshares and their spears into pruning hooks. Nation will not take up sword against nation, nor will they train for war anymore." This passage signifies that war will be absent in those heavenly days to come, but there is also a hint of work. The weapons that were once used for war are now being repurposed for working creation as it was in the beginning.

WHAT THE BIBLE SAYS ABOUT HEAVEN

Let's look at some of Jesus' teachings about the Kingdom of God for further examples. When faced with the overwhelming need among the sick and diseased, he addressed the disciples and said, "The harvest is plentiful but the workers are few. Ask the Lord of the harvest, therefore, to send out workers into his harvest field" (Matt. 9:37b–38). Or what about the parable of the talents found in Matt 25:14–30? The land owner entrusts a large sum of money to three men so that they might work with it and increase it while he's gone. Notice the response to the man with the five talents and the man with the three talents after the owner returns from his trip. Both of them doubled the amount of money that they had received and the master told them, "Well done, good and faithful servant! You have been faithful with a few things; I will put you in charge of many things. Come and share your master's happiness!" (Matt. 25:21). Notice that it says he will put them in charge of many things. He gave them more responsibility. Although it is hard to draw too much from this text because it is a parable and we cannot say for sure that Jesus intended to elude to the concept of work in heaven, it should cause us to consider that perhaps there is more in store for us than we have been imagining. Perhaps heaven will be more that sitting around for thousands and thousands of years. After all, Paul in First Corinthians 2:9 quotes Isaiah 64:4 when he wrote, "However, as it is written: 'What no eye has seen, what no ear has heard, and what no human mind has conceived'— the things God has prepared for those who love him—."

This realization that heaven may include activity and work shouldn't be feared. Before the Fall, work was good. Have you ever done a job or completed work that completely energized you? I believe that this is a glimpse of what work was meant to be. Unfortunately, in this fallen world, it can't be like that all of the time. But I believe that we can catch glimpses of it. When I teach, I feel energized and feel a deep connection to perhaps what God created me to do and be. However, we live in a society in which we are required to make money so that we can pay for shelter, food, clothing, and transportation, just to name a few things.

HEAVEN'S ECONOMY

It's also interesting to note that a formal "retirement" system wasn't even introduced into the world's economy until 1889.[2] America didn't adopt social insurance until 1935. With this new form of social insurance, retirement became a reality for more people than just the rich. Today in the twenty-first century, retirement has

2. http://www.ssa.gov/history/age65.html

become an art. There are a plethora of strategies and companies that exist to help you "retire well." Many of us develop long-term plans so that when we retire, we can do it in a way that allows us to live a comfortable life with little to no work effort.

Let's go back to our earlier thought that our brain allows our presuppositions, experiences, and cultural influences to fill the information gaps that we have. Because we often understand God and heaven through the filter of our own experiences and culture, I believe many Christians view heaven as a sort of eternal retirement plan. I've heard people talk about how they've "put in their time" during their earlier years and now it's the next generation's turn to do the "work" of the ministry. Although we may be able to retire from the American economy, I firmly believe that we don't retire from God's economy. Think of Abraham and Sarah. They were called to start a new nation when they were old and barren. God could have come to them earlier in their lives, but He didn't. God used Abraham and Sarah's wisdom and life struggles with bareness to begin a nation that would birth the messiah and the church that we know today. Retirement isn't a feature of God's Kingdom.

Talking to the Jewish leaders about his Father in John 5:17, Jesus said, "My Father is always at his work to this very day, and I too am working." God's Kingdom is always active, in all stages of life. In every year of our life, we have the opportunity to grow deeper with God and allow the Holy Spirit to transform us more and more into the likeness of Jesus. This is one of the amazing graces of God that we have an open door to pursue him any time. It is through this opportunity that we are preparing ourselves for the next life. Our current life is not the prize, nor do we achieve the prize during our time here on earth. This is why the idea of a spiritual retirement is invalid. We never rest in this life because our entire life, from birth to death, is a preparation period for eternity.

GROWING INTO HEAVEN

In *The Great Divorce*, C. S. Lewis tells about a man who takes a bus to heaven and is given the opportunity to check things out. Once arriving, he realizes that heaven isn't a very comfortable place.[3] In fact, it's very uncomfortable. The grass is stiff and sharp to his feet. We then find out that heaven is an uncomfortable place for him because his spirit is not attuned to it. His life was not spent on spiritually forming his soul to the things of God so when he arrived in heaven, it wasn't familiar to him. In similar fashion, the things that we invest in spiritually are preparing us for. . . something special. If we are focusing on growing deeper in our relationship with God and spiritually forming our souls for eternity, then I believe that when we get to heaven, there will be a familiarity to it. I also believe it will be exponentially greater than we could have ever imagined (see First Cor. 2:9 again), but there will be a sense of familiarity to it because we had a relationship with God on earth.

Have you ever had a long distance relationship or perhaps met someone through the Internet? Although you were communicating with that person through the Internet or by letter, your communications opened the door to a deeper level of relationship that you didn't have before. You got to know each other in a way that didn't exist before starting your correspondence. Then, when you finally met each other in person, there was already a sense of shared relationship and feelings for each other because of your long-distance experience. Similarly, we are currently in the midst of a long-distance relationship with Jesus Christ. We pray and communicate with God, and his Holy Spirit resides in us, but we have not seen him face-to-face. One day soon, though, we will be standing before his presence for the first time in physical form. When you do meet him, what will your thoughts be? Will you think about all those things that you shared through your long-distance relationship? Or will you be anxious because you never "wrote back"? Or, you just never could find the time in your schedule to develop the relationship because you were too busy to pray.

As mentioned previously, Dallas Willard rightly said that we are all being formed by something. For every person, spiritual formation is inevitable and unstoppable. The real questions are, what influences are forming your spirit and what is your spirit

3. Lewis, *The Great Divorce*.

being formed into? Is your soul being formed and prepared for a place such as heaven? Or is your selfishness and lack of care for the things of God preparing your soul for another place? Perhaps heaven would be a very uncomfortable place for those who are not practicing the things of God in this life. Francis Chan, in his book *You and Me Forever*, made a statement that still sticks out in my mind. He said, "I can't wait to die!"[4] Although I understand that he is illustrating his perspective of the importance of death and eternity, it still caused me pause when I first read it. His statement is a shocking reminder about what is important in this life. Chan argues that we lose an eternal perspective in marriage and family. We get so caught up in the stresses and values of this world, we can lose sight of what we are working toward, heaven! So in essence, Chan can't wait to die because that is where it all begins. Our eternal work with Jesus simply begins at death!

When we consider our discussion about having work to do in heaven, I wonder if those who have retired from spiritual activity in this world will be ready to get back to work in heaven? Perhaps those who are doing the work of the Kingdom of God here on earth will enter into a sense of familiarity when they get to heaven. Although I don't know the specific types of work we'll have in heaven, I do know some things about what it will be like. It will be just. All workers will receive the same and fair compensation based on the worth of the soul and not what they can "produce" (Matt. 20:1–16). There will be no more sorrow in heaven, and no tears will be shed (Rev. 21:4). The work will be full of joy and meaning. We will be in good company! We will be able to walk in the presence of God. The glory of his presence will be the light in which we work (Rev. 21:23). We will not be able to escape his presence, and that will be a good thing.

4. Chan, *You and Me Forever*. 133.

PREPARING FOR THE END OF THE WORLD (NO ZOMBIES INCLUDED)

So, how does apocalyptic spirituality tie into all of this? I believe that the intention of the book of Revelation is to remind us of all the good things to come. There will be some transitional pains in the process when justice is served, but we find ourselves back in paradise with the Tree of Life as if the story has started all over again. Yet, it seems that the church gets too stuck on the transitions to heaven. We get so carried away with how it's going to happen that we don't spend enough time in chapter 21 of Revelation. As the church, we must not get stuck on the details of the Day of Judgment because regardless of how many maps you own of the book of Revelation or how many different theories you've studied, you will never know when, how, and who. Besides, that is not what God wants us to focus on anyway. He asks us to be ready, to work on our souls, and to spiritually attune our spirits to the ways of the Kingdom of God, so that one day when we're there, we'll have a sense of familiarity to it and already be doing the work of the Kingdom. Only, it will be far grander than anything we could have imagined.

As the bride of Christ, we need to spend more time preparing ourselves for heaven and less time worrying about how end-time events are going to happen. If this life is the bride of Christ preparing for the wedding, then eternity is the beginning, the marriage relationship. We need to be teaching the church what the Kingdom of God looks like, how it operates, and how to have a long-distance relationship with the host, Jesus Christ. If you were asked to attend the most amazing party that ever occurred, would you spend all your time determining the type of vehicle that was going to pick you up and the route you were going to take, or would you spend your time imagining what the party would be like? The church has spent so much time fantasizing about how the Kingdom of God will be ushered into the world, that we've lost the passion for the most amazing party that has been promised to us. Historically, people have committed grave atrocities and misled countless people by focusing on secondary issues, and for what cause? War, injustice, and selfish ambitions will not bring heaven to our doorsteps any sooner. In fact, it may push it that much farther out of our reach.

A healthy apocalyptic spirituality seeks to live a life on earth that will be lived in eternity. Jesus alluded to such a type of spirituality when he said in the Lord's Prayer: "Your will be done, on earth as it is in heaven."[5] A healthy spirituality will value the things of God such as love, joy, peace, patience, kindness, goodness, faithfulness, gentleness, and self-control.[6] I find it ironic that so many of those who proclaim their "end-time" theories lack the core values that describe the true character of Christ's church. Many end-time promoters endorse war, impatience, intolerance, unfaithfulness, selfishness, and a lack of self-control. Can such attitudes prepare us for eternity? It satisfies our current desires for sensationalism, but it is spiritually bankrupt and only satisfies the fleshly need for information and entertainment. Yet, when we focus on the Kingdom of God according to the teaching of Jesus, we can develop a spiritual formation that will properly prepare our hearts and souls for eternity.

Many in the church have forgotten about the paradise that awaits us. It isn't a paradise because of what it offers us personally, but because it is a place that values the things of God. Heaven does not change because of what we desire, but we desire heaven because that is where God dwells and his Kingdom exists. So let the church desire the things of God in this life as well as in the next. Let us proclaim in the world today the good news of the gospel of Jesus Christ. The news is good because the Kingdom of God is at hand and can be experienced in great measure today. Then, one day, we will know it in full. May the church live out a healthy apocalyptic spirituality by striving to practice the life awaiting for us in eternity where there is no retirement, and the work is good and fulfilling. May the church experience the long term relationship with the Creator until the day it meets him in full. Let us not

5. Matt 6:10.

6. The fruits of the Spirit found in Gal 5:22–23.

be distracted with the unknowing details of the end of the world and instead focus upon the eternity that will follow. A new and fuller life awaits us, and we need to prepare our hearts and spirit for our departure. Until that time arrives, we have much work to do.

8

On Earth, As It Is in Heaven

He will wipe every tear from their eyes. There will be no
more death or mourning or crying or pain, for the old
order of things has passed away.

—Rev. 21:4

SO THEN, HOW SHALL we understand a book like Revelation? Do
we ignore it until the day comes when we are persecuted and need
a sign of hope for ourselves and our loved ones? Do we interpret
it literally, using the symbols and terminology with which we
are most familiar to squeeze it into the mold of our choosing so
it becomes relevant to our lives? Of course, the answer to both
questions is an emphatic "No!" I firmly believe that there is a way
to understand the book of Revelation that gives us the space not
to understand it literally—that is, not employing a naïve literal-
ism that uses inconsistent interpretive methods that speculatively
project symbolic meanings into apocalyptic texts. We may not be
able to interpret the exact meaning of all of the passages found
in this wonderful book, but we can use it to grow spiritually and
become more and more like the "KING OF KINGS AND LORD
OF LORDS" (Rev. 19:16) central to its message. Let's dive in and

look at several passages, not to focus on dates and times and imagery, but to discover what we can about our Savior, his mission to restore a fallen world, and how we can grow in faith and Christlikeness while we await his return.

Historically, Revelation has been interpreted many different ways. It has been interpreted allegorically, symbolically, historically, and literally. The method that I am suggesting the church adapt is richly allegorical, but also practical for today. Claims to allegorical interpretation are *not* a claim that the book of Revelation is untrue or talking about unreal events. On the contrary, references to allegory involve the genre, which then requires consideration of the full historical and literary contexts of the book of Revelation.

The challenge with a literal perspective is that it views Revelation in an informational approach that doesn't create space for spiritual formation; it also does not admit its repeated use of allegorical (and symbolic) interpretation as a part of what is meant by "literal."[1] It leaves us in a place where we are merely waiting for the literal events to occur. When we can approach the text allegorically and get to the heart of what the book of Revelation is trying to communicate to the church, we are able to see God's heart and intention for his people who are suffering. When understanding the text allegorically, we can also leave room for future fulfillment and be content with not knowing the details of the end of the world.

When we rethink the end of the world, we are not choosing to read Revelation as a literal piece of information that is not relevant to us until the day or hour that a series of events occur. Rather, we are choosing to read Revelation in a way that helps us to come to a deeper understanding of God's heart for his suffering people. When we understand apocalyptic spirituality and how it influences the way we think about the end of the world, we can give greater care to how we understand Revelation so that it will

---

1. Even so-called literal interpreters of Revelation appeals to allegorical and symbolic interpretations of the text, arguing that the genre requires it. But are not such literalistic interpretations guilty of inconsistency, at best, and hypocrisy at worst?

influence our spirituality and perspective of the end of the world in a healthier way. Let me use a visual to illustrate:

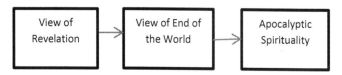

Figure 1. **How interpretation affects spritual formation**

For example, if people have a literal view of Revelation, then they will see the end of the world as a series of events that will happen someday, and it will affect their spirituality in that they may simply be waiting and watching for signs. However, if you were to view Revelation in an allegorical way, then you would have an understanding that Jesus will come again someday. But the details and signs aren't as important as developing our hearts and spirits because the spiritual formation of our hearts is what will be judged in the end. How you view Revelation interpretationally will affect how you view the end of the world and, in turn, will affect how you are preparing yourself for the Day of Judgment.

This chapter is designed to help Christians and churches rethink the end of the world by understanding the nature of apocalyptic spirituality. We will talk about several of the more common images in Revelation and get to the heart of what God is trying to do on behalf of his suffering people. This is not an exhaustive account of the book of Revelation, but merely several examples to illustrate how we can rethink the end of the world by understanding the nature of apocalyptic spirituality. Once we understand the heart of what is being communicated, we can take that and allow it to spiritually form us and gain a better perspective on God's design for the end of the world. Once we understand God's mission in the world and his desire for restoration, we can then co-labor with God and help to usher in the restoration that Revelation communicates to the church.

THE SEVEN CHURCHES OF ASIA MINOR—
REVELATION 2 AND 3

Regarding the letters to the seven churches in Asia Minor found in chapters 2 and 3, most Bible scholars interpret the churches to be real people in ancient history. In other words, Jesus directed John to write letters to actual churches so he could commend them for the things they were doing right, as well as indicate areas where they needed improvement. These two chapters are probably the easiest to use for creating spiritual formation in the church today because they speak directly to brothers and sisters, address real problems, and provide real solutions. We need to remember, however, that the imagery Jesus used to describe himself and address each church was relevant to the people of that time and location. That is, they could readily understand the language and images used to address them because they were familiar with the terminology and concepts. Today, however, when we attempt to understand these chapters using our own understanding and the context of our own time and place in history, things oftentimes go terribly wrong.

We just don't get it! For example, some people believe these two chapters relate solely to the original first century churches and have nothing to do with the church today. Consequently, they see no reason to relate what Jesus is saying in these chapters to today's churches. Premillennial Dispensationalists interpret the letters as historical dispensations; that is, each church represents a specific time in church history. In this way, the seven churches constitute prophetic stages in church history that forecast the coming of a future apocalypse. Neither of these views necessarily offers any "spiritual food" for building up the church today. But, there is another way to view them, one that can provide us with a wonderful picture of the Savior who is the head of the body, the church, and how he deals with his people, regardless of the time and location.

T. Scott Daniels offers a view of these chapters that can bring spiritual understanding and formation to our doorstep. According to Daniels, the key to understanding these passages is found in WHO the letters are addressed to, namely, the angels of the churches, not the people in the churches.[2] So, who are these angels? He argues that the letters to the churches aren't just to groups of people living in the listed cities, but they are to the collective spirit that is created by all the members in the church. Daniels stated,

> The seven angels of the churches to whom John writes are neither disconnected spiritual beings nor merely a colorful way of describing nonexistent realities. Instead, the term "angel" signifies the very real ethos or communal essence that either gives life to, or works at destroying, the spiritual fabric of the very community that gave birth to it.[3]

Daniels continues, "I am now convinced that churches, because they are a communal body, have an essence or collective spirit that is at work either aiding or hindering the life-giving work of the Spirit of God."[4]

With this understanding of the essence of the letters to the seven churches, it becomes easier to see how we can understand chapters 2 and 3 in a spiritually formative way. When we look over the shoulders of the seven churches of Asia Minor and read their "mail" (found in these two chapters), we can discern what Jesus (the Head of the church) saw in them from a spiritual perspective and how it formed and shaped them. By studying their letters and hearing Jesus' warnings to them, we discover that we're often guilty of the same errors. We can then try to step back and pray for discernment to see what kind of letter Jesus would write to our church. Perhaps you could even create a safe place in your church for collaboration and have several members from different perspectives within the church write letters from a "Jesus perspective" and have each member read them aloud. Chances are the things that keep popping up in the letters and discussion will be issues that can be taken to the next level of consideration and prayer. Before you begin this exercise, however, you should begin with

2. Daniels and Mouw, *Seven Deadly Spirits: The Message of Revelation* , 17.

3. Ibid.

4. Ibid.

prayer and ask Jesus to open your spiritual eyes and walk among your church. Ask him what he sees and to give you the humility to accept his words to the "angel" of your church.

THE 144,000

Two passages in Revelation talk about a group of 144,000 people. Chapter 7 identifies them as being marked on their foreheads with a seal of protection before any harm was brought upon the land, sea, or trees. Later, in chapter 14, God gives them a special song to sing to the LORD that no one else knows. Who the 144,000 are has been a controversial passage over the centuries. However, perhaps a better way to view the passage is not to try to determine who the 144,000 are but to see God's heart as he relates to them. He cares deeply for them and doesn't want any harm to come to them.[5] They have a special song that only they can sing before the throne of God. This passage of the 144,000 being sealed on their foreheads reminds me of Genesis 4, where God placed a mark on Cain, a mark of protection from harm that could befall him because of his murder of Abel. Even though Cain had committed a grievous sin, God's mark of protection would keep others from taking his life. By seeing and understanding God's heart in the passage, perhaps we can begin to understand His plan to restore all things instead of simply viewing Revelation as a roadmap of where we fit into the big picture of the last days. Much of the imagery in the book of Revelation is actually references to Old Testament imagery. This is another reason an allegorical understanding of Revelation is helpful, because Revelation uses allegory to communicate its message to a suffering church community.

So, if I were to pray through the book of Revelation, when I get to the 144,000 in chapters 7 and 12, I would approach it in a spiritually formative way. For example, after seeing God's heart to protect the "servants of God" (Revelation 7:3), I could spend time in prayer asking God to protect my brothers and sisters in Christ

5. Conversely, the "mark of the beast" (Rev 13:18) ends all divine protection, temporarily and eternally. See the next section of this chapter.

around the world who are suffering and being persecuted for their faith. The believers in Southern Sudan are a perfect example of those who currently need our prayer support. Or if you are passionate about social justice, then you could pray for the safety of the thousands of children taken into slavery each year around the world. Pray that a "mark of protection" would be placed on their foreheads to protect them from the evil that surrounds them. Then, as you pray for the swift justice of God to come and rescue them, find ways to co-labor with God in taking action to restore the victims and help bring justice to those who are being oppressed.

THE MARK OF THE BEAST

In our generation, the "mark of the beast," identified in Rev. 13:18 has been a wildly sensationalized image and is known to many people whether they have read Revelation or not. The mark of the beast can be seen as a mark of oppression that is forced upon the people by the "beast." Revelation 13:16–17 says, "It also forced everyone, small and great, rich and poor, free and slave, to receive a mark on his right hand or on his forehead, so that no one could buy or sell unless he had the mark, which is the name of the beast or the number of his name." So without the mark, they are marginalized and suffer from being excluded from society. According to these two verses, people who accept this mark will be able to participate in the world's economy, but they will not be spared God's wrath for following the beast over the Lord.

So how do we see God's mission in the world through the mark of the beast? It can be very symbolic of actions in the world today. Every day we are faced with the temptation to worship something in the world instead of the God in heaven. For some people, this takes the form of money, possessions, and unhealthy relationships. Although these things may not leave a visible tattoo on your body with the number 666, it can leave a mark on you spiritually. You can become dependent on the unhealthy idol instead of depending on God to provide all your needs. When I read this passage, I remember Jesus' words when he said, "Man shall not live on bread alone, but on every word that comes from the mouth of God" (Matt. 4:4). Our life does not depend on the world's economy, but rather on God's economy.

How can you apply what you know about our Heavenly Father to this passage? First, you can pray that you will be able to resist the idols and possessions that may tempt you to depend on them for peace, joy, or happiness. It is not God's desire that we give our allegiance and commitment to something other than Him alone. He is a jealous God (Exod. 34:14). We can remember the Old Testament story of Aaron's golden calf; those who turned away from God and put their hope and faith in an idol were greatly disappointed in the end. The things of this world will pass away, and Revelation reminds us that we have a lot more at stake here in our earthly existence than may appear.

THE MILLENNIUM

Of the many images and symbols in the book of Revelation, the concept of the millennium has been one of the more popular. It has become a cornerstone for various interpretations, such as pre-millennial, post-millennial, and a-millennial eschatologies. Some interpretations include a literal one thousand year reign of Jesus Christ on the earth and try to describe it in some fashion. But few provide a spiritual understanding of the reign of Christ. Christians in the first century were already being persecuted by Rome, which was quickly approaching its millennial celebration in 248 CE. The fact that Rome would celebrate its one thousand year reign is hard to ignore when hearing Revelation speak of a millennial reign of Jesus Christ. Without the original context, it is hard to understand what is occurring when we read this passage two thousand years after it was written. Although we may never fully understand the original meaning, we can see God's heart in it and what this millennial imagery represents to his suffering people.

In Revelation 20, John sees a vision of a millennial reign of Jesus Christ and the imprisonment of Satan until the one thousand years has ended. The imagery seems to parallel the reign of

Rome for its millennial birthday. The early Christians would have compared the millennial reign of Christ spoken in Revelation to the millennial reign of oppressive Rome. Like Satan, Rome has reigned and oppressed the people of the earth, and Caesar has rivaled God by demanding that the Romans address him as Lord. However, Revelation gave hope that Jesus Christ would have his own millennial reign, and the serpent, Satan, would be oppressed and imprisoned. There would be a spiritual vice versa, however, because Jesus Christ would emerge victorious after he defeated Satan, subsequent to his release, after Jesus' millennial reign.

It is easy to see how the millennial reign can be understood in a literal way, but how can we understand this concept in a spiritually formative way? As we live our lives in this world, we simply cannot miss the evil powers that seek to misguide and oppress people. Similar to Rome, these people and governments put the needs of the leaders above the needs of the people. This passage reminds us that God sees the oppression of these people in the world, and I believe the church needs to be aware and active of them as well. I believe we, the body of Christ, do the world a disservice when we write off Revelation as a future fulfillment, but fail to open our eyes to the evil and oppression in the world today.

So, what can we apply in a spiritually formative way when we consider the millennium? Revelation 20 gives us a glimpse into God's heart for those in the world who suffer from oppression. Again, we see those with the mark of the lamb come forth and actually reign WITH Christ for the millennium (Rev. 20:4). Think about this; those who were being oppressed by the power of Satan are now the ones reigning with Jesus—and their oppressor, Satan, is chained and himself justly punished. Jesus has turned the tables. Justice has come, and even though many have died in direct opposition to their oppressors, they arose first in the resurrection and had all access backstage passes to the millennial reign of Jesus Christ. There is a sense of justice here for which we yearn when we see the innocent in this world die through the horrific violence brought upon them by the nations of this world.

Pray for those who are oppressed as you co-labor with the Holy Spirit because God's heart is to free those who are enslaved in this world . . . even if it isn't until the next life. Pray for the oppressed, and work to free those you can. Rejoice that at the very least, they will see God's justice in the next life.

THE NEW EARTH

One of the most exciting passages for me is Rev. 21, which gives us a glimpse of what John recognizes as the New Earth. He says that the Old Earth has passed away, and before him is a new earth with no sea (Rev. 21:1–2). It is interesting that John notices that there is no sea because in ancient times, the sea was a mysterious and ominous place. They didn't have the technology to explore the seas and the depths of the seas like we do today. Ancient Israel didn't have the capacity to know what was in the deep, dark waters. They didn't know about the angler fish or other mysterious creatures that existed in the oceans. With so much uncertainty of the waters, the seas were a symbol of chaos and uncontrollable forces. I hear of similar fears from people who don't like riding horses because they have a mind of their own, and you can't fully control them. Ancient Israelites felt the same way. With this in mind, it brings even more richness to the way Jesus calmed the sea before the disciples. They were amazed because Jesus tamed the untamable. We also see earlier in Revelation that a sea of glass was before the throne of God. It's not that the sea was literally made of glass, but that the water was so calm and void of chaos that it was like glass. So, we see here in the new world that the waters aren't just calm; they are gone. The uncertainty is gone from the picture. We receive confirmation of this peaceful estate when we read Rev. 21:4, "He will wipe every tear from their eyes. There will be no more death or mourning or crying or pain, for the old order of things has passed away."

What a marvelous picture of the new earth (Rev. 21:1–4)! Yet, the question remains, where did the old earth go? It is interesting to note that there seems to be more biblical support for it being the same earth, just "flipped." Extreme Earth Makeover perhaps. Just as in the last chapter where we discussed a more biblical understanding of heaven, John is now eluding to the new earth as a "remodeled" world. The old world is still the same creation from Gen. 1:1, but God has redeemed it in full. Isaiah speaks of swords being beaten into ploughshares (Isa. 2:4), and Scripture talks about the redemption of creation (Rom. 8:22).

So, what do we do with this passage? Do we simply wait at the end of the dock and wait for this new earth to appear? How do we view the earth in light of Revelation and God's mission? This is where I believe we can be the most practical with Revelation. If we truly do not know when Jesus will return, then we have to be honest and say that it could be another two thousand years. I am pretty sure that if you asked Paul when Jesus was going to return, then he would have dismissed the idea that people would still be waiting two thousand years later. With this in mind, there is much we can do while we wait for Jesus to return.

This perspective reminds me of the apocalyptic parable of the talents (also called the parable of the bags of gold) found in Matt. 25. The master gave the talents to the servants and left on a journey. When he returned, he judged the servants based on what they did with the talents in his absence. He rewarded the work and diligence of the first two servants who doubled their talents, but he condemned the one who buried his talent and did things his way. In a similar fashion, we have been left *talents* with which to work while the Master is away. What will we do with them? It doesn't take much with today's technology to see the tragedies and injustices occurring in the world. When we pray the Lord's Prayer and ask that God's will be done on earth as it is in heaven, do we really want that to happen? If so, then what are we doing to bring a stronger presence of God's kingdom to the earth?

Imagine an earth where the Kingdom of God is busy multiplying the talents left to them while they wait for the Master to return. Some citizens of heaven are planting trees to prevent environmental devastation while simultaneously taking care of the space on which God has left us to live. Other citizens are using their earthly resources to fight the sex trafficking that oppresses people and robs them of their basic human freedoms given to them by their Master. Yet other citizens of heaven are looking around their communities for "neighbors" who need to be loved and reminded that there is a Master who sees their trials and tribulations and is working to make things right on the earth. And if they don't see it in this life, then they will experience it in the next. Imagine a church that lives in anticipation of the return of Jesus but lives out each day renovating this world into the Kingdom of God that is to come. I believe the "angel" to that church would be very excited!

Jesus provides a glimpse of what the end looks like, not so we can predict when it will happen, but WHAT will happen and how we should be prepared for it. If we know when He will return, then most of us would succumb to the temptation not to be ready until we believe the end is near. If you know when he's coming, then you won't be ready when he's not coming. Perhaps, instead of a roadmap of how the world is going to end, we have been given a glimpse into God's heart for his people and what the Kingdom of God looks like here and now.

The book of Revelation is a spiritually apocalyptic book that reminds us that one day Jesus will return for us! It is a signal of hope that flashes across the sky and reminds us that Jesus will return and set all things right. It gives us a hope that one day evil will be destroyed, and justice will finally prevail. Slavery will end. Violence and abuse will end. All pain and suffering will cease. He will wipe every tear from our eyes, and we will be able to experience eternal joy and peace unhindered.

9

What Are We Waiting For?

> He will wipe every tear from their eyes. There will be no
> more death or mourning or crying or pain, for the old
> order of things has passed away.
>
> —Rev. 21:4

I BELIEVE THAT THE history of apocalyptic spirituality should be
weighed with just as much seriousness and concern as other major
historical influences. We've seen in chapter 5 how people's view
of the end of the world directly affected their lives and even the
lives around them, and in rarer cases . . . the world. So, why do
many churches avoid educating, or even addressing, the influence of apocalyptic spirituality in Christianity? If we abandon the
teachings and application of Revelation to the sensational confer-
ences and the Internet, then the church neglects a major part of the
Christian life: the anticipation of the return of our King.

APOCALYPTIC DISCIPLESHIP

So what does it look like to live a balanced, healthy apocalyptic
spirituality? With a healthier spiritually formative understanding

of Revelation, the question still remains: How does apocalyptic spirituality affect discipleship in the twenty-first century? I believe that we can learn a lot from the example of Paul on how to live in anticipation. However, I believe that we can also learn from Paul's experience and realize that it could be another two thousand years before Christ returns. Therefore, we need to rethink the end of the world and the possibility of living to an old age before Jesus returns. We must learn to live in a space where we greatly anticipate the return of Jesus and all the things it will bring with it, but we also must learn to live in the possibility of experiencing a long life and a natural death before he returns. This chapter will talk more about how to live in that tension.

Like Paul, mission-minded disciples are running the race hard and want to dive across the finish line when it appears. These same disciples love God by spiritually preparing themselves for the return of Christ at any moment, and they love their neighbors by living their lives as if he may not return for another two thousand years. To ignore our responsibilities to our neighbors and the environment because we don't think we will be on this earth very long is irresponsible and selfish. We do great at preparing for our retirement and 401k, but we don't prepare the following generations spiritually. Ironically (or hypercritically), do those who claim the imminent return of Jesus have a 401k retirement plan? If so, then how much does the theory of their advocacy match the practice of their lives?

Throughout certain parts of church history, we have been looking at Revelation backwards. What I mean is that oftentimes the church has been waiting for Jesus to come to them rather than working towards God's final mission of restoration that we see in Revelation. Apocalyptic spirituality is a built-in facet of mission-minded thinking because the church is looking outward rather than inward. This simply means that the mission-minded church is looking around them to see what God is doing and getting in on it rather than waiting for people to come to the church before Christians minister to those in need. The dangers and misunderstandings of Revelation often occur when you open up this last book of the Bible and start reading with this question in mind: How does it relate to me? When we start with this presupposition, suddenly imaginary scenarios and wars are concocted to begin to make the book of Revelation relevant to our current situation, and we have to wait for a series of events to occur until suddenly we are in the midst of the trials and tribulations of Revelation. We can bend the book of Revelation to fit our lifestyles today. However, a mission-minded perspective of Revelation is all about bending ourselves to God's great narrative to redeem this world.

Therefore, just as the mission-minded church seeks to relate to the world, when we enter into Scripture to see what God is doing, we begin to see a different narrative. Suddenly, we are no longer trying to find out when and where all the apocalyptic imagery will happen, but we are starting to ask questions like: What is God doing here? Does he really feel that way about injustices like poverty, racism, and bigotry in the world? This mission-minded understanding of the end of the world allows us to see an overall view of Revelation and the agenda of the vision that is given to John: hope, peace, and restoration of all creation.

Jesus' disciples need to understand the spiritual formation of Revelation so they can synchronize their hearts with the heart of God. However, this can be a challenging task when many people in the church are skeptical of this book and make an effort to steer clear of it. Pan-millennialism (it will all "pan" out in the end) is becoming a much larger group in the twenty-first century. Although pan-millennialism isn't necessarily a bad thing, it seems to be one of the few options available to people who do not want to chase cultural signs of future fulfillments. The book of Revelation is an incredible part of Scripture that helps us to see God's "big picture." To leave it out or neglect it would be like cutting the last chapter of a murder mystery novel. You never discover "who did it." It would be like cutting out the last movie in the *Lord of the Rings* trilogy: You'd be left in a world filled with evil, with little hope or vision of victory. It would leave us in a place of confusion and uncertainty.

Stop to think for a moment: How would your faith be different if you didn't have Revelation in the Bible? In the absence of apocalyptic spirituality, Christians could become bored and complacent once they've experienced a certain amount of faith. They have lost the vision for the endgame and start dispersing because the church has merely become a social event with no long-term vision. Even carrying our cross daily loses meaning if we fail to understand the long-term goal: to be transformed into the likeness of Jesus. Otherwise, carrying our cross daily feels like torture and uncomfortable without the rallying cry of why we do it day after day after day. The book of Revelation holds the standard high in the daily battle and creates an apocalyptic spirituality that empowers us to keep fighting, to keep carrying the cross because, in the end, God wins.

HEALTHY APOCALYPTICALLY-MINDED CHURCHES

The spiritual formation of Revelation gives us a framework for a deeper understanding of the crucifixion, death, and resurrection of Jesus Christ. If we just preach about the fall and redemption of humanity, then we are missing out on two major parts of the story in the Christian faith: creation and restoration.[1] The church has led people to believe that once you accept Jesus as your savior and have been forgiven of your sins, you have arrived and are simply waiting for Jesus to return. However, Revelation reminds us that we are working toward the restoration of all things, a new heaven and a new earth. He will make all things new (Rev. 21:4). We see this message begin in the letters to the seven churches in Asia Minor. Jesus wants them to be restored. In fact, one church was waiting, and they fell asleep! Jesus is walking among them and saying, "Wake up!" As I look at many churches today, I have the same feeling that he is walking among the pews shouting, "Wake up!" The end hasn't come yet, and there is still much work to be done!

The church needs to spend more time teaching and preaching in Revelation because it reveals to us the finality of God's mission

1. Lyons, *The Next Christians: The Good News About the End of Christian America*, 51.

in the world. When we tell people the end of the story, they have something to work toward. When they see that God desires to restore things and make all things new, suddenly the church is in the business of co-laboring with the Holy Spirit in helping to restore people on earth today. The church is not waiting to be restored; God is working on restoring people *now*. Heaven will be a greater extension of what is already happening in the world today. However, if people believe that all there is to Christianity is being forgiven and just trying to be good till death or Jesus returns, then they are not understanding God's plan for restoring their souls.

C. S. Lewis, in *The Great Divorce*, talks about a man's journey to heaven and how uncomfortable it is for him because his soul is not attuned to the environment.[2] However, when the main character accepts God's love and allows himself to be restored into who God created him to be, he suddenly finds that heaven is an amazing place and very comfortable. In the same way, in this life, we are allowing ourselves to be restored to prepare ourselves now for the eternal fellowship with our Lord and Savior. Spiritual transformation is simply allowing ourselves to be restored into the person that God created us to be. If we allow that transformation to occur, I believe that when we arrive, heaven will have a faint sense of familiarity to it because we are helping to shape the Kingdom of God on earth *today*. It will be much grander and clearer than it is now, but I believe there will be a taste of familiarity because we felt the Holy Spirit's presence on earth as God was working in our lives all along.

So, how can we be a disciple of Christ as we live in this world but anticipate the next? I believe that we can go back to Paul and glean from his example to us. Despite Paul's understanding that Jesus was coming back soon, he never felt compelled to gather people and go and wait on a hill for Jesus. In fact, the nearness of Jesus' return was more motivation to help the church go deeper in Christ. Think about it; he believed that Jesus could be back at any moment, and he is worried that some Christians are still immature in their faith and drinking "milk" when they should have moved

2. Lewis, *The Great Divorce*.

onto eating meat (1 Corinthians 3:2). Paul was not about getting people simply to finish the race. For Paul, becoming a Christian was just the beginning. He himself commented that he had not yet attained the prize of perfection in Christ (Philippians 3:12). He was still running the race with all effort to complete the race strong and tumble across the finish line.

However, some Christians, in preparation for the return of Jesus, are only concerned about getting people across the threshold and not helping them to go deeper. Part of the problem that I have with apocalyptic evangelists is that they speak of the doom and gloom of Jesus' return, but offer little application for life today. Phrases like "turn and burn" or "repent or go to hell" keep surfacing. However, is that all Christianity is about? Those phrases communicate that you need to become a Christian to escape eternal punishment. However, I don't believe that is the full gospel. The good news is that you can be restored from the brokenness you are experiencing in this life. Jesus' return is about the final reconciliation with our Creator and being renewed. Reconciliation is a painful experience if we have a lot of brokenness left.

HEALTHY APOCALYPTICALLY-MINDED LEADERS

The harvest is plentiful, but the workers are few (Matt. 9:37). Perhaps the American harvest has been even more lacking because the church has put tight restrictions on what defines a person as a Christian harvester. I remember one of my first charges as a pastor of a small church in rural Indiana. As a full-time college student and part-time minister, I was swamped with ministry and studies. So, I simply asked the administrative board to consider hiring a youth pastor or finding a volunteer to share in the work. The patriarch in the church was the first to speak, and I still remember his response: "We pay YOU to do the ministry. We don't need to bring someone else in for help." That was also the last comment from the board on that topic.

Somewhere along the ecclesiastical journey, we taught the church a very narrow view of Christian service. The focus was a need to convince people of their sinfulness due to the fall and proclaim the blood of Jesus that redeemed them. So, the church hired lots of evangelists and preachers to accommodate these two aspects of ministry. Gabe Lyons, in his book *The Next Christians: Seven Ways You Can Live the Gospel and Restore the World*, states:

> Is evangelism really the only use for the millions of church goers in our culture? Now, put restoration back into the story. Instantly, you've created millions of jobs for all the "unemployed" and bored Christians in the church—jobs they can get excited about.[3]

In some circles, the church has been led to believe that only the pastors or church staff members do the work of the ministry. However, a mission-minded perspective rightly identifies that all believers have a purpose and calling to do ministry in the Kingdom of God. This "priesthood of all believers" (1 Pet. 2:5) was a key emphasis of Martin Luther and subsequent Protestants. But in practice, this reformational emphasis can be lost by churches. The church needs to be in the business of engaging the mission of God and producing not only evangelists and disciples, but also park rangers, social workers, teachers, bank tellers, doctors, nurses, advocates for the abolition of slavery, forest workers, environmental specialists, and the list could go on and on. Consider how Craig Van Gelder and Dwight Zscheile advocate churches as God's most immediate representation of God's Kingdom here-and-now:

> The church is a window to the reign of God. How people view the church is how they view the Kingdom of God.[4]

Many people have seen a building full of sin and forgiveness and rejected a truncated gospel. When we focus only on the sin and redemption ministry of God's mission in the local church, we begin creating buildings and structures that serve the agenda of saving people from a fiery hell rather than plugging into God's

3. Lyons, *The Next Christians: The Good News About the End of Christian America*, 160.

4. Van Gelder and Zscheile, *Missional Church in Perspective, The: Mapping Trends and Shaping the Conversation*, 106.

grander mission of healing and restoration for heaven and earth. Again, consider the words of Van Gelder and Zscheile in describing a mission-minded church:

> In an instrumental view, the church primarily exists to do something; the character of its being is neglected. What remains is a purposive ecclesiology in which the wider framework of God's Trinitarian agency recedes. Its eschatological dimension, or the way in which the church embodies the future toward which God is drawing all humanity, is unfortunately underemphasized. The church exists merely to accomplish something on behalf of God.[5]

HEALTHY APOCALYPTICALLY-MINDED MISSION

Restorative eschatology[6] is underemphasized, if at all, in turn or burn churches because the church exists mostly to do "something" instead of conforming to what God is doing. However, if you bring back the larger mission of God, namely, to redeem and restore all of creation, heaven, and earth, then suddenly the gospel becomes whole again and very relevant to the world *today*. Guder and Barrett say:

> Missional leadership is shaped by the revelation of Jesus Christ. In the incarnation, through Jesus' life, death, and resurrection, what was hidden from before creation is now out in the open: God is bringing all things into a healed oneness under the authority of Jesus. Jesus brings a new social reality, a healed creation. By implication, leaders, in the name of Jesus, guide the community of God's pilgrim people as the sign and witness of what has happened to the world in and through the incarnation of Jesus Christ. In Jesus the reign of God has become present. In his actions and resurrection he demonstrates that God is acting incarnationally to redeem and renew

5. Ibid, 106–107.

6. Eschatology is the study of the end of the world.

creation. He announces that the future of creation is directed toward this community of God's reign.[7]

This quote by Guder and Barrett, taken from the book *Missional Church: A Vision for the Sending of the Church in North America* explains well the role that mission-minded leaders can have in the church today. In a culture that hungers for transformational experience, incarnational leadership will be crucial for successful ministry in the mission of God. Church leaders must be guides on how to bring restoration to themselves and their own family, as well as to the world. This restoration can be visible through relational, environmental, and social venues. The church needs to open its doors and let the people out to bring healing and restoration to a broken and hurting world. We have kept people locked up inside the church for too long.

Leaders must be studying the Scripture, especially the book of Revelation, which shows us the final acts of restoration to better understand the mission of God with a new perspective. Teaching and re-teaching will be an important task for the church because the church needs to rethink the end of the world. We must go back to the basics to see what God is doing in the world and discover where we are located in the storyline. Guder and Barrett remind us of the importance of mission-minded leadership:

> Jesus indicated that his mission was formation, fulfillment, and empowerment of a new community, a new people created and sent by God. By implication, leadership finds its most significant definition in the same mission.[8]

A healthy understanding of apocalyptic spirituality in a mission-minded church focused on a restorative eschatology will create disciples that eagerly anticipate the second coming of Christ because it will be the arrival of the final restoration of all creation. However, these disciples will not be content to stand on

---

7. Guder and Barrett, *Missional Church: A Vision for the Sending of the Church in North America*, 185.

8. Ibid.

the docks waiting for this day to come, but they will be active in their communities and aware of God's mission in their local and global contexts. They will teach and preach the spiritual formation of Revelation as a book of hope and discovery as they share and participate in God's plan for restoration. Lives will be changed because they took time to rethink the end of the world and decided to make a difference in the world today *while* they wait for the Jesus.

10

Conclusion
This Is the End

> They were looking intently up into the sky as he was going, when suddenly two men dressed in white stood beside them. "Men of Galilee," they said, "why do you stand here looking into the sky? This same Jesus, who has been taken from you into heaven, will come back in the same way you have seen him go into heaven."
>
> —Acts 1:10, 11

THE GOAL OF CHRISTIANITY is to be made into the likeness of Jesus Christ. Apocalyptic spirituality plays a major role in our spiritual formation and the church. Jesus' emphasis on how to be ready for his return involved the spiritual formation of loving God and loving one's neighbor.

Paul's emphasis on spiritual formation was about helping the church to go deeper in faith with Christ under an apocalyptic shadow. Christians can often become side-tracked with only trying to save souls and getting them to enter into heaven, but that is not God's only mission for the church, and it is not the apocalyptic spirituality that we see in the New Testament.

The mission of God is interested in restoring the world and all that is in it. A church that focuses exclusively on sin and forgiveness doesn't easily know what to do with Revelation because it has ignored the restoration aspect of the gospel. Instead, many churches that focus only on the sin and forgiveness aspect of Christianity look for signs and sensational events because there is no proper framework to understand God's plan to re-create the world. Throughout history, the church has waited for Christ's return as a form of deliverance from a socioeconomic situation; however, perhaps God had something bigger in mind. The church has had to do eschatological gymnastics to make it fit the agenda of the society. Instead of allowing Revelation to impact culture, the church has tried to use culture to impact Revelation.

A healthy church that understands God's mission in the world sees the larger picture from creation to final restoration in Rev. 21–22 and determines how it can play an active part in God's plan. It understands apocalyptic spirituality in Revelation and God's plan to bring restoration to all of creation and, therefore, acts accordingly. Consider the following description of a church that practices a healthy apocalyptic spirituality in response to God's mission:

> God sees brokenness in the world and seeks ways to address it. It can spot darkness and show up with whatever light it can bring. Few people would be able to claim that the church was judgmental. It would be full of grace, giving the recipient of its love the benefit of the doubt. It would look for the best in people, seeing the image of God in everyone it encounters, even when the darker side gets the best of them.[1]

This is the church for which the world yearns and what I believe Jesus intended the Kingdom of God to be. We are challenged to rethink the end of the world because we have missed out on God's mission and have chosen to bend Revelation to our mission. Revelation and apocalyptic spirituality are not about understanding

1. Lyons, *The Next Christians: The Good News About the End of Christian America*, 73.

the signs of the times. It is about the final restoration of making all things new—individuals, society, and all of creation. "The End is Near" should be a joyous expression of peace and hope. However, the church has made it into an apocalyptic doomsday that says we should be fearful of and relatively passive until Jesus' return.

So, I challenge you who are part of the church: Rethink the end of the world. Preach and teach about God's mission to restore the world and make all things new—spiritually, physically, and in all ways. Let Jesus' return be an event worth anticipating because of the joy, peace, hope, and restoration it will bring. In the meantime, we have work to do, reflective of God's calling upon us as believers. We are the kingdom of God on earth. Let us co-labor with the Holy Spirit in continuing the work of restoration to the earth and its inhabitants, with the knowledge that one day it will be *fully* restored in final redemption when the Son of Man comes to us on the clouds.

What a day that will be!

Bibliography

Allison, Dale C. et al. *The Apocalyptic Jesus: A Debate.* Santa Rosa, CA: Polebridge, 2001.

Ambinder, Marc. "Falwell Suggests 'Gays to Blame for Attacks.'" *ABC News.* http://abcnews.go.com/Politics/story?id=121322.

Augustine of Hippo. *City of God.* Translated by Henry Bettenson. London, England: Penguin Classics, 2003.

Boyer, Paul. *When Time Shall Be No More: Prophecy Belief in Modern American Culture.* Cambridge, MA: Harvard University Press, 1992.

Chan, Francis. *You and Me Forever.* San Francisco: Claire Love, 2014.

Collins, John Joseph. *The Apocalyptic Imagination: An Introduction to Jewish Apocalyptic Literature.* Grand Rapids: Eerdmans, 1998.

Cran, William, and Ben Loeterman. *Apocalypse!: The Story of the Book of Revelation.* VHS. Directed by William Cran and Ben Loeterman. FRONTLINE, 1999.

Carol Delaney. *Columbus and the Quest for Jerusalem.* New York: Simon & Schuster, 2011.

Daniels, T. Scott, and Richard Mouw. *Seven Deadly Spirits: The Message of Revelation.* Grand Rapids, MI: Baker Academic, 2009.

Dyer, Charles H., and Angela Elwell Hunt. *The Rise of Babylon: Sign of the End of Times.* Wheaton, IL: Tyndale House, 1991.

Fowler, James W. *Stages of Faith: The Psychology of Human Development and the Quest for Meaning.* New York: Harper Collins, 1981.

Guder, Darrell L., and Lois Barrett. *Missional Church: A Vision for the Sending of the Church in North America.* Grand Rapids: Eerdmans, 1998.

Hagee, John. *Four Blood Moons: Something Is About to Change.* Brentwood, TN: Worthy, 2013.

Harrington, Daniel J. *Matthew.* Sacra Pagina. Collegeville, MN: The Liturgical, 1991.

Humphrey, Edith M. "Ambivalent Apocalypse: Apocalyptic Rhetoric and Intertextuality in 2 Corinthians." In *The Intertexture of Apocalyptic Discourse in the New Testament*, edited by Duane F. Watson, 114. Atlanta: Society of Biblical Literature, 2002.

Bibliography

Josephus, Flavius. *The Jewish War: Revised Edition*. Translated by G. A. Williamson. London: Penguin Classics, 1984.

Keener, Craig S. *The Gospel of Matthew: A Socio-Rhetorical Commentary*. Grand Rapids: Eerdmans, 1999.

Knight, George R. *Millennial Fever: A Study of Millerite Adventism*. Nampa, ID: Pacific, 1993.

Lewis, C.S. *The Great Divorce*. New York: HarperCollins, 2010.

Lindsey, Hal, and Carla C. Carlson. *The Late, Great Planet Earth*. Grand Rapids: Zondervan, 1970.

Lyons, Gabe. *The Next Christians: The Good News About the End of Christian America*. New York: Doubleday, 2010.

McGinn, Bernard. "Apocalyptic Spirituality: Treatises and Letters of Lactantius, Adso of Montier-En-Der, Joachim of Fiore, the Franciscan Spirituals, Savonarola." In *The Classics of Western Spirituality*, edited by Richard J. Payne. Mahwah, NJ: Paulist, 1979.

Murphy, Frederick J. *Apocalypticism in the Bible and Its World: A Comprehensive Introduction*. Grand Rapids: Baker Academic, 2012.

Newbigin, Lesslie. *The Open Secret: An Introduction to the Theory of Mission*. Grand Rapids: Eerdmans, 1995.

Osborne, Grant R. "Matthew." In *Exegetical Commentary on the New Testament*, edited by Clinton E. Arnold. Grand Rapids: Zondervan, 2010.

Powell, Marvin A. "Weights and Measures." In *Anchor Bible Dictionary*, edited by David Noel Freedman. New York: Doubleday, 1992.

Rudolf, John Collins. "An Evangelical Backlash Against Environmentalism." NY Times. http://green.blogs.nytimes.com/2010/12/30/an-evangelical-backlash-against-environmentalism.

Tacitus. *Annals*. Translated by Cynthia Damon. London: Penguin Classics, 2013.

Van Gelder, Craig, and Dwight J. Zscheile. *Missional Church in Perspective, The: Mapping Trends and Shaping the Conversation*. Grand Rapids: Baker Academic, 2011.

Willard, Dallas. *Renovation of the Heart: Putting on the Character of Christ*. Colorado Springs: NavPress, 2002.

Williams, A. W. *The Life and Work of Dwight L. Moody: The Great Evangelist of the 19th Century*. New York: Cosmic Books, 2007.

Winthrop, John. "A City Upon a Hill." In *A Modell of Christian Charity*, Collections of the Massachusetts Historical Society, 3rd series, 7:31–48. Boston, 1838.

Wright, N. T. *Surprised by Hope: Rethinking Heaven, the Resurrection, and the Mission of the Church*. Nashville: HarperCollins, 2009.

42169335R00066

Made in the USA
Lexington, KY
10 June 2015